THE SECRET TEACHER

DISPATCHES FROM THE CLASSROOM

First published by Guardian Faber in 2017

Guardian Faber is an imprint of Faber & Faber Ltd,
Bloomsbury House, 74–77 Great Russell Street,
London WC1B 3DA

Guardian is a registered trade mark of
Guardian News & Media Ltd,
Kings Place, 90 York Way, London N1 9GU

Typeset by Faber & Faber Limited
Printed and bound by CPI Group (UK) Ltd, Croydon CR0 4YY

This paperback edition published in 2018

A CIP record for this book
is available from the British Library

ISBN 978–1–78335–127–5

FSC
www.fsc.org
MIX
Paper from
responsible sources
FSC® C020471

2 4 6 8 10 9 7 5 3 1

To the kids and teachers, with love

Tell all the truth but tell it slant –
Success in Circuit lies
Too bright for our infirm Delight
The Truth's superb surprise
As Lightning to the Children eased
With explanation kind
The Truth must dazzle gradually
Or every man be blind –

Emily Dickinson

When I was a child, I spake as a child, I understood
as a child, I thought as a child: but when I became
a man, I put away childish things.

1 Corinthians 13:11

Author's note: This book is not literally true.
The school and the individuals in this book are
composites; they owe much to the pupils and
teachers I have worked with at different schools
but I've changed identifying characteristics in
order to protect their privacy.

A glossary is provided to guide the reader in the
way teachers and kids talk among themselves and
to each other.

Contents

Contents

PART ONE

1

Phoenix

The alarms went off at 5.30 a.m. I had set three – one on my phone, one on the travel alarm and one on the radio – so when they all went off it was like an air-raid warning. Amy was incandescent; she had been able to get up and out every day without it being such a palaver. She put the pillow over her head and shouted, 'You're only going in for induction! What are you going to be like when you actually have to teach? Just get out!'

That's nice, that is. I was doing this for her, after all. (She hated it when I said this. OK, maybe it wasn't all for her. Maybe for her and Dad. And Granddad. And me, kind of.) I was abandoning the world of bohemian flakery and uncertainty to become a man of purpose. A man of solvency. A man who wore M&S jumpers.

I hurriedly put on my suit, tie and turquoise M&S jumper in the dim, cold hallway. It had been so long since I had tied a tie, I throttled myself as the knot shrank to the size of a peach stone. I went down to the kitchen and tried to eat some toast, but my stomach was churning. I paced up and down, checking my briefcase repeatedly for the bounty from my 'Back to School' Ryman ram-raid: yellow Post-its; Moleskine (hello, Hemingway); USB stick (empty); pink Post-its; multi-coloured dividers; orange Ryman Foolscap Square Cut Folder; Ryman Essentials

Lever Arch A4 neon-blue enormo-file; lip balm; Travel Card; green Post-its.

I wonder if Hemingway used Post-its. 'For sale: baby shoes, never worn' would fit on one. Go bullfight. Drink sangria. Write Post-it.

Lesson #1
Always Have a Stash of Post-its
in Your Pocket.

Whenever you find yourself at a loss for a Plenary – the last few minutes of a lesson when the kids have to summarise what they have learned – just stick a Post-it on every desk and tell them to write something down. The kids stick them on the board on their way out. I got my job purely on the strength of a jazzy Post-it Plenary. *Year 9: Writing to Advise*. I said, 'Write me some advice on a Post-it and put it on the board as you go out.' One said, 'Get an Xbox.' Another, 'Get a new tie.' Another, 'Come work here. It's the best school.'

I squeezed my feet into my new brown brogues – déclassé to the City boys, raffish to the Inner-City boys – winced and headed out. There were lots of grown-ups around, heading off to proper jobs, looking at their glowing phones, like monkeys pointing mirrors at the sun. I felt my vertebrae unfurling as I marched along with purpose and pride.

Here I go. To work. With my briefcase. Full of Post-its.

I found myself walking alongside kids on their way to school and gasped with joy.

4

Here they are! My base metal that I will turn to gold with my alchemy. My empty vessels, waiting to be filled with pure knowledge!

Buses hacked up great clumps of kids in Puffa jackets. The Puffas swam together into a large school, moving in formation. I was caught in the current, surrounded, and as the *swish swish swish* intensified, I began to panic.

This is it. Snuffed out before I have begun. Drowned by Puffa.

The Puffas darted right, sucked into the plughole of a school's gates. I stood on the pavement, bedraggled and relieved.

I walked along elegantly bombed streets, passing Volvos, delis, and an eternity of jerk chicken, until I reached a coffee shop with distressed architrave – a ghostly reminder that it was once a butcher's. Outside, hungover young men in stripy Breton shirts were tapping on Mac-Books and scratching their half-beards. Yeah, I remember being one of those half-men. Half man, half jellyfish. A budget centaur. Hopeless, purposeless, dangling men, scratching around in the desperate freelance hardscrabble twilight. No structure, no routine, no human interaction, no dignity. Drinking endless coffees, sending thousands of emails, tapping into the void. Whole days spent trying to come up with catchy puns. The last one I did was for a competition to win a bed. I stared at the screen all day. Late in the afternoon, after a revelatory brownie, I came up with 'Beddy Prize'. My boss didn't get back to me. I sent him a follow-up email explaining that it sounded like 'Beddy Byes'. I never heard back.

I'd like to stick 'Beddy Prize' on a Post-it on his face. And I'd say, 'Look at me now. No longer using my linguistic mastery to sell shit to morons, but selling Language, Culture, Art, Philosophy, Sociology, the Mysteries of Existence, the whole shitshow, to kids who really need it.'

As I turned the corner, a large girl burdened by a huge rucksack was bent over, moaning in pain.

One of my charges. A youth in distress. My first act of salvation.

I asked if she was OK. 'Yeah, I'm all right. My pussy hurt, dat's all.'

I entered the newsagent's, clocking the sign that read NO MORE THAN 3 SCHOOLKID AT A TIME, before being confronted by a pair of tanned women who were buying bags of Haribos.

'Only way to keep them under control at this time of year,' said one.

'Why do we bother? I mean, once they've done their tests we should just let them go on holiday. I feel like I'm some kind of gameshow host: "And now for another round of Who's in the Bag?"'

I bought another pen and a banana. The newsagent pointed the banana at a half-naked woman on the front page of a tabloid.

'I banana her,' he said.

I looked at him, uncertainly.

'You teacher?' he asked.

'Yes. Yes, I am,' I proudly replied.

'Nice teachers at your school. I want to banana them.'

I pushed my thumbs up in the air and muttered an awkward 'Cheers', and left the shop.

The world is truly vulgar. I must beat it back. My classroom shall be a bulwark against the tides of corruption. An Edenic sanctuary. And lo, I shall deliver the Innocents unto Purity and Enlightenment.

I followed the two women up the road. A guy in a passing car wolf-whistled and made a gesture that seemed to indicate that he too wanted to banana them. I thought back to the teachers I had at school: old dishevelled guys with hairy ears and egg on their ties you would see wandering the streets talking to themselves. Here was the new breed: beautiful, tanned, coiffed, corporately dressed young men and women who walked with dynamic swagger to the sexiest job in town.

At the end of the road, in a crater surrounded by council estates and terraced houses, throbbed a shimmering glass palace. Well, most of it. Half of the old school building and half of the new stood each side of an enormous chasm. On one side of the chasm tottered the 1960s brutalist concrete comprehensive, grey and mournful; on the other thrust the twenty-first-century panopticon, shiny and garish. It looked like a spaceship had crashed into an NCP car park.

Outside the gate was a shiny zinc sign, embossed like a Silicon start-up's, with the school's name, the Head's name, a large space for an OFSTED quote, and the School Motto: 'QUESTING FOR EXCELLENCE'.

The Receptionist buzzed me through and handed me a laminated card, which I struggled to fix to my lapel as

I read the three letters that were to define me for a year: NQT. Newly Qualified Teacher.

'I thought it said RIP!' I said.

'I give you those on your way out,' she said. 'Now you have to go and have your finger scanned.'

'My finger scanned? What did I do wrong?'

'You gotta use it to open doors, photocopy, eat lunch. You need your finger to do everything round here.'

In the Canteen, a long queue of new staff waited to be registered. Embossed. Uploaded. One of the chefs was manning the till. She laughed at my nervous approach.

'It won't bite! Just put your finger on the scanner, darlin'.'

As I placed my finger warily on the scanner, a buzz of electricity rushed through my body.

Buzz.

I looked up at the screens hanging from the ceiling.

Buzz.

A graph appeared.

Buzz.

A pulse flickered.

It lives.

Having been validated, I walked out to the playground feeling discombobulated. Maybe this was because 'DIS-COMBOBULATED' was the Word of the Day, and had been flashing on the screens. More likely, it was because I was beginning my new job when everyone else seemed to be finishing theirs. I had come in for the final week of the summer term to learn the ropes, but everyone else was in Summer Wind-Down Mode. Sixth formers lay on the grass. Tieless teachers in sunglasses drank tea nonchalantly in patches of sunlight. Sweaty boys with their shirts conspicuously untucked bashed a tennis ball all over the playground with abandon, while joyous girls hopped over skipping ropes. It reminded me of the video for 'Me and Julio Down by the Schoolyard'.

I stood in a huddle with the other NQTs, swapping war stories from teacher training. We had all taken different routes – PGCE, GTP, TeachFirst, Schools Direct. No matter which route we had taken, we all had to have experienced at least two different educational environments. This usually meant one nice place and one, *ahem*, 'challenging' school. You could tell instantly from the way new teachers discussed their placements how they really went.

'My first placement was at Lady Margaret's. Which was lovely. So lovely. Really lovely.'

My first tour of duty was a private school, where all the kids and staff were really polite and nice to me, and I taught mindfulness on the cricket pitch at lunchtime.

'Then, for my second placement, I was sent to St Swithun's. It was . . . good. Challenging, but good. I definitely learned a lot.'

My second tour of duty was in Helmand. It was hell. I'm still suffering from PTSD. I couldn't control the kids, who were feral. Boys wanking in the playground over their phones. Sawing off chair legs at the back of the classroom. The staff didn't offer any support. I had to be parachuted out of there.

'Hi. I'm the other NQT in English.' A tense young woman shook my hand with brittle urgency. Before I could say anything, she bombarded me with a nervous spiel. 'How are you finding it? Where did you train? How was that? I knew someone there. Cat. Cat in Art? Where else? Oh, right. So how was that? Was it good? My second placement was great. I mean, really good. Outstanding.'

Oh, I've got your number, Little Miss Outstanding.

Our guide was a sixth former, who was among the most personable and confident people I had ever met. The tour of the old part of the school was brief and apologetic. We stood in an old classroom that had been cut in half, and gazed down at the men in hard hats shouting over the digging and drilling. Giant tendrils of steel wept from the floor, cascading over the chasm. Piles of old exercise books lay pell-mell around the shelves, stacked alongside old ravaged Ladybirds. Post-it notes sticking out of Arden Shakespeares fluttered in the breeze. Laminated posters with slogans like *WE ARE EXCELLIN!* slid perpendicularly from single blobs of Blu-Tack down the wall.

Then we toured the new building. It was like walking round a cruise liner: a vortex of steel and glass, surrounding atriums, gyms, music studios and science laboratories. Along every suspended hallway, screens blazed with photographs and graphs of sanitised success.

Every classroom was a fish tank, surrounded by high glass. Senior Managers looked into classrooms on regular 'Learning Walks' around the school, in order to establish there was no bad behaviour or irregular teaching taking place. The glass was occasionally obscured by sugar-paper presentations, olde-worlde epistles that had been dipped in tea for historical verisimilitude, poetry, slogans, Punctuation Pyramids and literary or motivational quotes ('To be or not to be' – Hamlet; 'You miss 100% of the shots you don't take' – Wayne Gretzky).

We walked on.

The silence.

There was only silence, purposeful silence, occasionally punctuated by the beeping of computers, photocopiers and security doors. And in every classroom, dynamic, beautiful staff were standing before dynamic, beautiful slides and happy, shiny pupils, caught in this palace of light.

On the stairs, where kids moved in silence in lines and there was not a moment of jostling – most behaviour issues start during transitions between lessons – there were poems, essays and photographs of authors, rappers and entertainers. Everything smelt vaguely of chlorine. 'Like a patient etherised on a table,' I thought, and then was confronted by a photograph of T. S. Eliot looking constipated. An image of a dusty, cracked landscape. Underneath, in tiny pencil lettering: *waste man*. A picture of a desert island next to 'Island Man' by Grace Nichols. A photograph of Sylvia Plath on black sugar paper; in silver Trebuchet:

I am silver and exact

The students' art, stark and beautiful: androgynous figures prostrate before broken trees; globular mouths wailing through fish-eye lenses; fists of defiance. At the bottom

11

of each of these *cris de cœur* were emblazoned the blue letters of the corporate sponsor of the school.

We descended into an atrium to admire the sofas and chairs.

'And these are our chairs. What do you think?' asked the sixth former, as if this was the highlight of the tour.

To be fair, they were pretty natty. The main body of the chair was transparent plastic, but they had these unforgiving white leather pads on the seat and back. Chairs that screamed, 'Sit on me! And work! And don't get up until you've finished!'

Standing in the middle of the atrium, looking up towards the glass roof, I felt the overbearing sense of being watched. I could be seen through the denuded library shelves; from gangways that laddered upwards to the roof; from the very seat of heaven.

Along a corkboard partition, the Head of History was putting up a poster of all the key events in English history: a timeline of all the kings and queens. Posters of Martin Luther King, Rosa Parks and Gandhi lay on the floor behind her.

'The sponsors are very keen on history,' she said, with a mischievous wink.

At the end of the tour, I asked the sixth former what he really thought of the school. (I mean, *really*.)

'It was the crucible in which my soul was forged,' he said. 'It saved my life.'

Back in the old building, the English Department was a comforting oasis of chaos. Amid the cascade of old essays, notes, sugar paper, tennis balls, boxer shorts, half-eaten granola bars and Zumba leggings were broken-spined copies of *York Notes to 'Macbeth'*, *The Poetry of Langston Hughes*, *A Guide to One Direction*. At the back of the room, by the window, perched the coffee machine on a table, dripping hypnotically into its tray. A murky puce liquid overflowed the brim, from which emanated a smell of dank cow juice, barely masked by perfume.

A portly middle-aged man stood imperiously, tea in hand, staring out of the window, surveying his dominion. The Head of Department in repose. Out in the playground, the Vice Principal was standing on a bench, gesturing with her arms like an air-traffic controller, bringing an entire group of unruly, sweaty kids, pumped and excitable at the end of break, to total silence.

'Like Caesar quelling the Gauls,' muttered HoD.

He pushed the button on the coffee machine for one last jet of water.

'Ah. The newbie is here. Ahhh. Delicate little wallflower.'

Lesson #2
Don't Sit Down in the Department
Until You Have Established Yourself.

Departments must accommodate many people, but tend to be small. Teachers get very possessive of their chairs. They have a brief window to plan or mark, and woe betide you if you are in their special chair when they charge in between lessons.

HoD ushered me into the seat he had just vacated as he grabbed a bunch of papers.

'Where's your Mentor? Teaching, is she? Silly cow. Sit down.'

He stared at my jumper.

'Ah. The old NQT jumper. The M&S classic. The first, and perhaps only thing you need to know about this job: never, *under any circumstances*, wear a jumper. Certainly not one as revolting as that. Pure hubris. A jumper will invariably become too hot within fifteen minutes of a lesson starting,' he said, stuffing a finger of Twix into his maw, 'and nothing will be more disempowering than taking your jumper off in the middle of a lesson, yanking your shirt out of your trousers and revealing your belly and potentially your pubes. But at least it isn't a cardigan.'

'Er . . . why's that?' I asked.

'That diktat came through the other day. NO CARDIGANS. You have been warned.'

He hitched up his trousers over his belly and belched, then watched me as I warily unpacked my Post-its.

'I'll wager a Cheese String that you don't use those all year.'

'Sorry?'

'Don't tell me you don't like Cheese Strings.'

'I don't think I've ever had one.'

'Jesus Christ. Where do they find you people?'

He took a Cheese String out of his desk and threw it at me.

'Your first assignment. Get your laughing gear round that. And describe the sensation, using a simile, or even better, a *WOW* word.'

I gingerly unwrapped the Cheese String and bit off the end.

'Like a . . . slimy eel.'

'Have a merit.'

A tall man with floppy hair and steamed glasses entered, threw his bag on the floor and declared, 'God, that newsagent is a filthy bastard.'

'This is Tom,' said HoD. 'He trained here last year and we decided to keep him on. God knows why. He'll take you under his wing. Show you the ropes. Keep you out of my face.'

'Mate, how's it going?'

Tom was a proper posho. Definitely TeachFirst.

The TeachFirsters tended to be 'bloody good blokes and top lasses' from the 7 per cent of the population who had been privately educated, and yet were imbued with a moral curiosity to find out how the other 93 per cent lived. If this had been a few years previous, some of them would never have been seen dead in a state school. They would have done the Milk Round in their final year of uni and snaffled a job at a Big Swinging Dick firm, but the Crash had put paid to that. Now they were part of 'the greatest generation to enter teaching', as Michael Gove put it when he was Secretary of State for Education. It felt good to be part of The Greatest Generation. A bit like it must have felt to fight in the Second World War. But there was always a nagging doubt that The Greatest Generation would stay until they decided to trade in those brown brogues for black ones and go suck Mammon's titties after all. The truth was that they were extremely well trained, and came armed with all the strategies, skills and energy you need to work in an inner-city state school. And they tended to stay in teaching, because they fell in love with it.

I looked over Little Miss Outstanding's shoulder at her laptop as she carefully tweaked the slides of a lesson. Images of storm clouds, blazing suns, snow; a grumpy face, a happy face; a sepia photograph of a man alone in a cell. In the corner, a small cartoon wizard waved a wand. A speech bubble in 72-point Comic Sans read:

What are we doing today??!!!

'Misery? Pain? Torture?' I guessed.

'Pretty much,' she replied.

She clicked on the rain cloud and rain fell onto squares that washed away to reveal the words:

PATHETIC FALLACY

She clicked again and the letters levitated back into the ether.

Fuck. Look at that shit. She's got proper production values. She's going to put me to shame.

'You can borrow it if you like. I've copied all my lessons onto the system,' she said.

'Thanks. Erm, yeah. I might do that.'

I put my empty USB stick into the computer and copied all her lessons onto it.

Why was I so lazy? I had done nothing on my training year. Literally nothing. Got eaten alive in Helmand, then got parachuted into a private school. They say it's like

16

going from walking on glass to walking on velvet. I got used to the luxury lifestyle. My standard lesson, which I gave most days to most classes, was to read *Bartleby the Scrivener* with them, then get them to write on a Post-it why they would prefer not to do their homework.

The Department door opened. It was like opening the boot of a car in which puppies had been trapped all afternoon. A litter of teachers leapt and licked and panted and barked and ran round and round in circles, chasing their tails. They talked very quickly about various extraordinarily monikered children – who were either wankers or geniuses – grabbed papers, spilt coffee and passed comment on my jumper. A young woman approached and beamed a smile that seemed to have originated in the first sunbeam that warmed the world. The 2nd in Department. My Mentor.

'Hello! Sorry, it's been mad. Have you met everyone? Ooh, nice jumper! Is it teal?'

A heavily pregnant woman shook my hand.

'Hi. You'll be taking over from me. Because I'm leaving. Obviously.' She handed me a bag, paper and a pen. 'Just write down any names of famous people and put them in the bag. I've got a double next and I'm getting quite bored of trying to do a charade of Kim Kardashian.'

'How do you do that without –'

'Exactly. I've got about twelve Malalas and Nelson Mandelas in here, but they just keep picking bloody Kim. And Wayne Rooney. It's rigged.'

'Shut up, you CRETIN!' The Head of Sixth Form charged in, shouting. 'Yes, you know who I am talking to!'

17

She shook her head as the door to the Department closed, still eyeballing the boy through the glass. 'Yes! You! I'm talking to you! WHERE'S. YOUR. ESSAY? WHAT DO YOU MEAN WHICH ONE? (Why do I bother. Seriously. I mean, look what I have to work with.) ON MY DESK BY THE END OF THE DAY OR I AM CALLING MUM. (What's he doing? He has no clue. Not one clue. Unbelievable. I might as well be talking to myself.) AND TUCK YOUR SHIRT IN!'

She turned from the window, took a deep breath, and surveyed me with gathering alarm.

'My God. That jumper is doing wonders for my hangover. Let me guess: one of the newbies?'

'Yes.'

'Have you had a Cheese String? Oh, good. Where did they find you? Apart from M&S? My God, look at him, he's shaking! Don't worry, I won't bite. Not you, anyway.'

I muttered something that was supposed to be witty but was, in fact, lame and inane. Dry as vermouth, she said, 'You're gonna get nuked.'

She looked at HoD, who nodded in agreement.

'Has he made you stack the books yet?' she asked.

'Er . . . no,' I said.

'God, what's going on round here? Going to the dogs. It is customary for you to spend most of this week in the stock cupboard. Don't be frightened. It can be fun in there. The Year 11 girls used to give blow-jobs at break'.

'Ahem. Not to us. And not any more,' said HoD. 'You need to get in there and stack all the texts neatly. It's a pigsty after a year of this lot taking books out and then dumping them wherever.'

'I will have you know, Sir,' Ho6 shot back, 'that every time I have returned a set of books, I have put them back neatly exactly where I found them. If you would care to peruse the shelves, you will see a full set of *Great Expectations* – from Year 8 Set 4, no less – and a full set of *Tempest*s from my cretinous 13s. You need to get in there sharpish, newbies. I have scheduled a nap on that yoga mat during my free this afternoon.'

Little Miss Outstanding and I entered the pigsty. The shelves and floor were scattered with textbooks, exercise books of every colour, plastic covers, French and Spanish dictionaries, a yoga mat and bottles of water. We decided that she would stack the *Jane Eyre*s and *Great Gatsby*s while I put all the exercise books into boxes. 'What an incredible smell you have discovered,' I said, but she didn't respond. I explained that I felt a bit like Hans Solo when he falls into the garbage chute with Princess Leia, but as soon as I said it, I realised it made it sound like we were destined to fall in love, which made the rest of our time in there pretty awkward.

After a couple of days of cleaning the store cupboard, I was told by HoD to go and watch some lessons. I followed a girl called Leila around, which was even more awkward.

Leila was in Year 9 Set 3, so I expected some trouble. The first lesson was Home Economics. Here we go, I thought. Year 9 troublemakers armed with knives and ovens.

The class filed in and stood looking at images of different types of bread on the board. We had to guess what they were going to make that lesson. Hands shot up; no one called out. Leila asked if it was pizza. The teacher corrected her warmly, telling her that we were going to make focaccia. After a brief written exercise, we put on aprons and chef hats, and arranged ourselves into groups, whereupon we began rolling pastry and dicing rosemary. The instructions were clearly written on the board and on a handout. The teacher had such control, she barely needed to speak. We put the focaccia in the oven, washed our hands, took off aprons and chef hats, and completed a written comprehension about the regional variations of focaccia in northern and southern Italy. Then we took the focaccia out of the oven; while it was a little bit soft, Leila and I agreed that it was delicious. She said she would try and make some for her mum at the weekend. For the Plenary, we stood behind our chairs and answered questions about how best to cook Italian delicacies.

We filed out into the playground. Leila ran off to join her friends, and looked back at me, giggling into the sleeve of her jumper, as I stood alone with my spongy focaccia.

Thanks, Leila. Just leave me hanging.

The rest of the day continued in the same vein. Power-Points in ICT, samba in Music, basketball in PE, the Battle of Hastings in History. In every class, the behaviour was immaculate, the group work perfectly marshalled, the tasks imaginative, the outcomes extraordinary. I was dazzled as entire classes wrote, put up their hands, drummed, threw baskets, retrieved facts, moved and thought in unison. It was like being inside a giant robot as it learned to breathe.

Then I observed some of my Department teach. Mentor was the Queen of Lesson Design. She made works of art on each slide, and spent hours on each lesson, carefully plotting each transition (the period between activities, when disruption is likely). Tom got them all going with drama, group work and debates. VP taught all the Set 3s and 4s because she had the most difficult kids at her beck and call. Every lesson followed the same formula, and they lapped it up. Ho6 and HoD, who had buckets of charisma, spent most of their lessons ripping the piss out of the kids and had them eating out of their hands. They had the all-important bantz. They were Bantosauruses. They qualified *bantum cum laude* from the Buju Banton School of Bantz at Bantchester University.

Lesson #3
Every Teacher Teaches in Their Own
Unique Way and Must Be Encouraged
to Find Their Own Style.

In most schools, there is at least one weak link, a teacher who makes you just think, 'Yeah, I'd have you', or 'If I was in this lesson, I would be bored shitless.' Not here. Here was a Cabinet of Many Talents. The true Jedis.

At the end of the week, HoD saw me looking overwhelmed in the corner of the Department.

'Freaked out, are you? You should be. Don't worry. They all feel like failures most of the time. We all do. Teaching is built for failure. Once you understand that, it's the best job in the world.'

On the last day of term, the whole school gathered for the Final Assembly for the Old Head. On the way up to the gym, I asked HoD why Old Head was leaving.

'Done his time. Brought us to the Promised Land. But he's the wrong sort for the New Regime.'

'Why?'

'He's a History teacher. A human. Who talks to the kids and is interested in them. He wears cardigans.'

'Who's going to replace him?'

'Well, that, my friend, is a sad tale we must save for winter. This will be a very different place next year. You'd better be prepared. I'm not sure I can help you with the Brave New World because I'm not sure I understand it myself.'

Old Head approached the dais at the front of the gym. He cleaned his glasses with the arm of his cardigan, then raised his hand with graceful solemnity.

'Pax.'

Pure silence.

'That is how my old History teacher used to begin every lesson. My History teacher who made me want to teach. Teaching is a noble profession. Perhaps the noblest there is.'

A cough. A whimper. A sob.

'To the staff, I say farewell. We are a happy Band of Brothers. We happy few. We have been together for many years at this wonderful school. I know many of you feel uncertain at all the changes. Do not fear. Your New Head' – he turned to acknowledge a man in a black Armani suit at the end of the row of Senior Managers on the stage – 'will lead you to bigger and better things.' New Head stared implacably, raising one foot so we could see the sole of his black brogue. 'You are on the brink of a very exciting new chapter in the school. You have brought us to the precipice. Don't lose faith. To the kids, I say: I have taught all over and the one thing I have learned is that "kids are kids are kids". But there are no kids like you. I shall never forget you.'

Some teachers sobbed into their hankies. Others were unmoved; they glared at the kids, who didn't know how to react: some cried, some laughed, some did both simultaneously, bending over and shaking, disrupting the whole row. The disruptors were swiftly disappeared.

HoD looked along the line of sobbing teachers and whispered, '*Après moi, le déluge.*'

Old Head wiped the tears from his glasses as the school Gospel Choir sang 'All You Need Is Love'.

At the end of the day, I went to see the Head of HR and signed up for the Golden Handcuff contract, which guaranteed I would work at the school for at least three years. 'That's you tied up!' he said, as he stuffed large pencils with kitten-head erasers into his fluffy purple pencil case.

I walked over to the gate and placed my finger on the scanner with pride.

The Secret Teacher

Buzz.
It lives.
And so do I.

2

Imperial Death Stare

The summer passed quickly. Amy and I went on a cheap holiday to Greece, mainly because I was going to have to teach the Greek Myths next term. Amy was already resentful that we could take holidays only at the same time as everyone else in the world; she now had to contend with my desire to go only where the books I was teaching were set.

'Come on, it'll be great!' I said. 'Next year, I'll be teaching *The God of Small Things*. We can go to Kerala.'

'I thought you said you would be teaching *Heart of Darkness*?'

'Congo will be fine by then.'

'Can't wait to go to Dunsinane in the winter,' she said, as she shielded her eyes from the sun with her Kindle.

I waved my edition of Greek Myths in the air excitedly. 'God, these myths are the nuts!' I shouted. 'The foundational stories of Western literature: simple pure gems with morals, adventure and magic. We're going to have so much fun with them.'

'Like what?' said Amy.

'I don't know . . . Like, we could make wings for Icarus.'

'Bit messy,' she said, as she squirted sun cream on her legs.

'I'm just going to read to them,' I said. 'It's what they need. They'll love it. I will be a carrier of the culture! I will lead them through "the vale of soul-making"! And they will never forget me!'

'I've never seen you so excited. I'm really happy for you. And proud,' she said, almost admiringly.

She kept saying that, but I knew she was still slightly disappointed in my career path. She was happy I had a proper job at last, but it wasn't a proper, proper job, one where I made some proper money. I kept telling her that all the old jobs had disappeared, and this was the only show in town. Teaching was different now. It was dynamic, sexy and well remunerated. I had Golden Handcuffs, after all. After centuries of being ignored and neglected, the Teacher was returning to the front of the class – like in France, where they are *professeurs*, or Japan, where they are *sensei* – someone who is a 'master' of their art.

On the first day of teacher training we were shown a grainy old photograph of a classroom in Ancient Sumeria: rows of stone, with a vacant space at the front for the teacher. After the apocalypse, only teaching will remain. Rows of stone facing an empty space surrounded by rubble.

'This is it now. I swear. I've found it. This is the thing. I will do nothing else for the rest of my life. These are the best stories. I'm at the best school in the world. And if this really is the Greatest Generation Ever to Enter Teaching . . . That means I am on track to become the Best Teacher Who Has Ever Lived!'

'Am I totally rubbed in?'

Autumn rolled in with the Back-to-School sales. I had everything I needed, mind. I buffed my brogues the night before the first day of term, and went to bed at nine o'clock. I lay awake most of the night. When I did finally go to sleep, I had a nightmare about trying to teach my first class. It was the generic 'Teaching with No Clothes On' dream, but it wasn't just my class who were laughing and banging their desks and pointing at me. I looked out of the fish bowl, and every pupil, teacher, Senior Manager and parent was doing the same. I tried to put my clothes on, but I couldn't move. I tried to speak; my mouth formed an O, but did not make a sound. A bubble of air drifted upwards as I slid down the glass.

On the first day of term, we had INSET. Our names were on a board at the entrance of the gym, as if we were attending a wedding feast. VP was directing traffic effortlessly. She was terrifying. Rumour had it she worked at the school every day from dawn to dusk, Monday to Saturday, and on Sunday she unwound by going paint-balling.

'HELLO, SIR!' she barked.

Who is she talking to?

'How are you, Sir? Settling in?'

Oh shit, she's talking to me. *I'm* Sir! Hello, Sir!

'Great, thanks, just great,' I choked.

'What do you think of the chairs?'

I looked at the chair carefully, swivelling it round on one leg.

'Go on! *Sit on it!*'

I sat down.

'Easily the most comfy chair I have sat in, in an educational setting,' I said, quivering, as I nestled my buttocks further into the cushion. I picked up my Planner, and started filling in my name on the cover. I felt seven years old. The teacher next to me leaned over.

'You won't use that again after the first week.'

The Senior Managers entered upstage left – a line of men in black Armani suits, carrying iPads – as we watched a welcome video, which looked like a 1970s Public Information film about crime. There was the old school, graffiti-daubed concrete slabs behind stoned hoodlums, a vision of brutalist failure. Cut to the new school: students of every ethnicity, smiling and laughing while they skipped, did their homework, played the trumpet. In all the pictures, the teachers gleamed and sparkled and looked like they had just been told the funniest joke of their lives, even if they were teaching Calculus.

VP strode forward and stared at us. Her presence thrummed.

'Some people say don't smile until Christmas.'

She clicked on a slide showing a chimpanzee with a frown.

'I say: Don't. Smile. At. All.'

The Music Department started giggling. She brought them to silence with a single glance.

'We believe in Back to Basics. These are the Non-Negotiables: Always have high expectations. Always be respectful. Always do your homework. Always be smart. Always do your best. Always do the right thing. Always walk the talk. Never give excuses. Win Win EVERY time.'

She sat and nodded to New Head, who approached the dais. He gave a Spanish teacher, who was still talking, a terrifying glare. She gulped, turned fuchsia, silenced.

Our Future Leader had come. Future Leaders were like TeachFirst for Senior Managers. They were young, ambitious, slick, and tended to come from the corporate sector; their mission was to improve schools, and they proved as successful as their TeachFirst counterparts. The improvements usually involved sweeping away all the dead wood, namely the Old Guard – the Not-So-Great Generations – with their unions, cardigans and old teaching methods, like reading, Chalk and Talk, and charm. I looked over at HoD, who had his head in his hands.

New Head clicked onto the next slide. A series of graphs and pie charts appeared. He recited the statistics: the percentage of A*–C at GCSE, what it was up from last year, and the year before; the percentage of A*–C at A Level, up from last year and the year before; the quantity of VA (Value Added); the league tables . . .

A new chart appeared: rows and rows of data, alongside names. One by one, he made teachers stand up. Those whose data had turned green – and who therefore were on track to satisfy their targets, like the Maths and ICT staff – were applauded. Those whose data had turned red – and who therefore were below target, like the History and RE staff – stood in silence. The Head of RE wept.

'And now, I would like to introduce a big drive that we are focusing on this year,' said New Head, in a doomed attempt to inject some levity. 'Can anyone guess what it is?'

A slide with images of fish and chips, Big Ben, Winston Churchill's victory salute, Emmeline Pankhurst, Justin Fashanu, Moeen Ali, curry.

'That's what I did last night!' shouted Mick, the jocular Learning Mentor.

'No.' New Head wasn't comfortable with the bantz.

'Britain?' asked a Geography teacher, tentatively.

'Good, Geography. I knew I could trust you,' said New Head. 'Yes. Britain. In every lesson, teachers need to try and include references to "British Values". What does Britain mean to you? I would like you all on your tables to come up with as many ideas as you can.'

I looked over Little Miss Outstanding's shoulder as she wrote 'toad in the hole' and '*Top Gear*' on a piece of paper. She got all defensive and said, 'Oi! Don't copy!' I had managed 'irony', 'Shakespeare', 'Germaine Greer', '*Planet Earth*' and 'The World Service', when Mentor leaned over to HoD and whispered, 'What's all this about?'

'It's just another fucking ridiculous initiative to make us all feel like we "belong",' shouted HoD, knowing it was loud enough for New Head to hear. 'Basically, they're all terrified that our lot are going to carry on going out and shanking kids from the wrong gang or blowing themselves up in the Middle East. Instil them with some moral fibre! Oh, sure. We'll sort that out! I'm not sure that showing them photos of fish and chips every morning is quite going to curb their *alienation*.'

Back in the Department, HoD took me through my classes. He scrolled through the headshots of all the students I would be teaching. It was like playing *Guess Who?*

'We only let you loose on Key Stage 3 to begin with. That's where it's at. Once you can handle them, you can handle anything. You've got a Year 9 Set 2 – tricky, but biddable – a Year 8 Set 3 – some difficult ones in there, on the turn – and a couple of Year 7s: Year 7 Set 1 (keep the parents sweet, don't let them get arrogant or they'll be insufferable). And then a Year 7 Set 4: totally unknown quantity. They've come from all manner of primary schools and the data's incomplete. They will be all over the place. No idea how to react to you or this school. There but for the grace of God go you. Take my advice: just go in, take the register, then slam the door, stick your fingers in your ears and sing "The Star Spangled Banner". That's what I used to do. Don't worry. We'll support you. I'll leave you to get acquainted with them all.' HoD clicked on an incomprehensible Technicolor splurge of data. Rows and columns of numbers and letters and pie charts were highlighted in red and yellow and green, accompanied by three-letter acronyms. Some had ticks next to EAL (English as an Additional Language); some next to SEN (Special Educational Needs); some had BH (Behavioural issues). And some had ticks next to all three.

Mentor entered and asked if I knew what I was going to do for my first Greek Myths lesson. I said I did.

'Great. Let's take a look.'

'Take a look?'

'At your slides.'

'Oh. No, I don't have any.'

'There are lots of lessons on the system you can use.'

'No, see, I was thinking of reading to them.'

'*Reading?*'

'Yeah, well, I thought, you know, what they need is books. They need to be read to.'

She looked at me suspiciously.

'Oh. OK. Well, let's see how that goes, shall we? Sounds great.'

My first lesson with Year 7 Set 1 went swimmingly. As I took the register, they replied, 'Good morning, Mr Teacher', in a cutesy Shirley Temple singsong.

Throughout the lesson, I thought there was a mosquito in the room, but it was just the ambient whine of keenness. Whenever I asked a question, all the arms in the room shot upwards and bent sideways; they looked like humpbacks arcing out of the sea.

I asked if any of them had read any of the Greek Myths before. Hands rocketed. They had read them, reread them, seen the play, acted in the play, watched the film, played the computer game. We discussed all their favourite myths. They asked if they could write their own, *PUH-LEEEAAASSSSEEE?* I said they could. They wrote as if it was a race and after about ten minutes all shouted, 'FINISHED! Can I read mine?' For the rest of the lesson, I sat at the desk at the front, while they read me stories. I felt like a child being put to bed.

Then I had the Year 7 Set 4s. I had my slide projected when they came in, with my name, the date, the name of the subject, and the classroom rules, underneath a generic photo of a stern teacher with a mortar board and cane I had found on Google Images.

They entered in dribs and drabs, looking confused but not appropriately scared.

I stared at them. And stared. And stared.

Once they were in their seats, I started to speak. There was a quiver in my voice. I cleared my throat.

'Write. This. Down.'

They settled down and managed to copy my name, the date and 'English' – they all tried to do funny adulterations to the 'i', like turn the dot into a heart or an explosion – before I took the register.

'Milosz?'

'Sir.'

'Mercedes?'

Does her dad drive one? Was she conceived in one? Maybe *she* drives one?

'Wa'gwan,' replied Mercedes in a gravelly growl which bespoke a lifetime of fraught experience, as she combed her afro assiduously. She was like an eleven-year-old Etta James.

'Yes, *Sir.*'

'A'right, Sir.'

'*Yes*, Sir!'

'YES, SIR!'

'Donnie?'

'Hmm?'

'Donnie? Are you here?'

'Here. Sir.'

'Saadia? Saadia?'

'Sir.'

'Salim?'

'Chika?'

A large, pale boy with a vacant stare stood in the doorway. A battered seal pup adrift on an iceberg.

'Can I help you?'

'Yeah. Is dis English?'

'Yes. Come in. You must be Kieran?'

'Yeah.'

Lesson #4
Any Kid Whose Name Begins with K
Is Bad News.

'Yes, *Sir*,' I said.

'Yeah.'

'No, that's what you say: "Yes, *Sir*!" Kieran?'

'Yeah?'

'Don't "Yeah" me! It's "Yes, *Sir*!" You're not in primary school now! And if you think you're going to "Yeah" me all year, you've got another thing coming!'

I can't believe I just said that. Where did my mother come from?

'OK, get to your seat. Now who has heard of the Greek Myths?'

Tumbleweed.

'No? OK, well, great. You're in for a treat, let me tell you. Nothing like them. The best stories ever written. So I will start reading and then we can discuss it. OK?'

Blank faces.

'OK: "In the beginning – way back at the beginning of time – the world was empty. There were no computers or phones or schools or uniforms or animals or birds or teachers or kids. There were only gods, who ruled the world from Mount Olympus, otherwise known as heaven, where they lived in halls of sunlight and cloud."'

Why are they giggling?

Check a few things on the sly, while I turn around to change the slide.

Belt. Check. Shirt buttons. Check. Tie. Check. Flies. Check.

Is something on my face?

'Er . . . what's so funny?'

There's definitely something on my face. Time for the 'sweep manoeuvre': a cough and a wipe across the face.

And we're back in the room.

'Anyone know who king of the gods is?'

'Me!'

'Jay Z!'

'Don't call out.'

In every classroom there was an Interactive Whiteboard, with magic pens that could be rubbed out with the click of a mouse. There were also old-fashioned Dry Erase Retractable Whiteboards, with old-school markers. I picked up a pen and wrote 'Zeus' on the board. With a plunging sense of horror, I realised I had written on the Interactive Whiteboard with an old-school marker pen. I desperately tried to rub it out with the interactive magic rubber; when this failed, I tried the old ragged cloth, but to no avail. Now 'Ze' would be on the board forever. Basic schoolboy error.

They're pissing themselves. Just read on.

'So Zeus – yes, Zeus, you see – "Zeus, king of the gods, decided he wanted some living creatures to play with, so he sent Prometheus and his brother Epimetheus down to earth to make them. Epimetheus made the animals, birds, insects and fishes. Then Prometheus made the very last creature of all." (Can anyone guess what it is? No?) "He mixed soil and mud and made . . ." (Anyone?) "First Man!" First person, I should say. The first human, basically.'

They're still giggling.

Try the Death Stare. Find a kid, and fix your eyeballs on them. A proper Death Stare can take anywhere from ten seconds to a minute. When you hear kids whispering 'Shhh! Be quiet!', and there is only one kid making noise and everyone is looking at that kid and telling them to shut up, then you know your Death Stare has been effective, and you can relax your eyeballs.

I swivelled and eyeballed Mercedes. She giggled louder. Then I turned to Kieran, who pissed himself. Soon they were all over the place, rolling around with laughter.

'What's so funny?'

'Nuffin.'

Mercedes buried her head in the inside of her blazer elbow.

'Just focus. Please.'

A bit of residual Death Stare. Then onwards.

'"But Man was naked and alone in a hostile world. Prometheus decided that First Man needed more. So he climbed up to heaven, where he stole a tiny sliver of fire from the sun.

'"You have done something very bad!" shouted Zeus. "You have given the secret of fire to those mud-men!"'

'You are mud-man!'

'Mud-man!'

'Waste-man!'

'You're waste, man!'

'Come den, fam!'

'Allow it!'

'Er . . . quiet, please! Settle down!'

Just plough on.

'"Not only have you given away something precious and divine, but now these silly mud-people will think they are gods! Do you think your pathetic creations are more important than us? I'll make you sorry you were ever made yourself!"'

They're still messing around. Time to lose it.

'I'll make you sorry that you were ever made yourself!'

What? What was that? *Did you just say that?* What the hell does that mean?

'I'll make you sorry you were ever born!'

Hmm. Bit better. Still a bit like Mother, but it's done now.

'How you gonna make me sorry dat I was born?' Kieran shouted.

He's got a point. Strange phrase. Don't try and explain it. Just move on. Quick! Make an example of him! Set a precedent! Make the earth shake with your fury! You are a god unto whom he must prostrate himself or risk eternal vengeance! Bollock him! Now!

'Is this how you behaved in primary school?'

'Yeah.'

'Is it?'

'Yeah.'

'And is this how you behave at home?'

'Yeah.'

Of course it is.

'If you think you are going to behave like that here, you've got another thing coming.'

Oh, Mother. You still here?

'What other thing is coming?'

'It's a phrase –'

Another weird phrase I can't explain. How am I supposed to teach English when it is full of all these inexplicable phrases? Just plough on.

'Sit up straight. Straighten your tie. Milosz, get your hands out of your trousers. Put your hands here! Here! Where I can see them! OK. I don't know what primary school you went to –'

Well, you do.

They started shouting out the names of their primary schools and which was better. Within moments, Mentor was at the door. In any other class, they would have shut up immediately. But they did not understand who she was or the power she represented.

'Whatever you learned in primary school, you can forget it.'

Really? What, all of it?

'You're in Big School now. For Big Boys and Girls. And we have rules. That you must follow. You sit up straight.

You don't fidget. You listen. You are polite. Read me number 3 on the list of classroom rules from the front of your book, Mercedes. Mercedes! Read me number 3.'

'I can't say.'

'Why?'

'It says "No calling out". How can I say it if I can't call out?'

'That's right: "No calling out". And if you can't do any of these things – Kieran, I'm still talking and I am talking to you; are you listening? Well, stop looking out of the window. And Milosz, take your hands out of your trousers –'

Slipping. I'm slipping into the quicksand.

'OK. Next person who fidgets is going out! . . . Kieran! Out!'

'What?'

'Get out! I've warned you enough times! Just get out!'

He continued his protestations. Mentor beckoned to him. And with that, he was disappeared.

'OK. Let that be a lesson to you.'

Yes, Mother. Well done. The first lesson you have taught.

'Let's carry on: "Zeus punished Prometheus by tying him to a cliff and sending eagles to peck at his liver forever." Can you imagine what that is like, Milosz? Can you? Having an eagle peck out your liver forever?'

'What's liver?'

'It's like dat steak and kidney fing,' said Donnie.

'Steak and what?'

'Kidneys.'

'Steak and kid's knees. What are you chattin'?'

They're all laughing.

'AH HAH HAH HAH HAH! LOLZZ!'

'MEGALOLZ!'

Shit, they're so noisy. With my door open, the noise is spreading out over the entire school. Shhh! Shut up! Single them out by name. It's the only way.

'Donnie. OK. Mercedes. All right. Calm down. Look, I want to get on. We need to read about the most beautiful woman in the world! Don't you want to know about the most beautiful woman in the world?'

'Is it about Beyoncé?'

'No, it's not Beyoncé. Even more beautiful than Beyoncé.'

'True say?'

'Naaaaaaah . . . No one. NO ONE is more beautiful dan Beyoncé.'

'Yes. Because Zeus had also made First Woman. Called Pandora.'

'PanDORA!'

'NAAAAHHHHHH . . .'

'Wahey!'

'Woo!'

'"PANDORA MARRIED EPIMETHEUS. He was devoted to her. He gave her everything she desired."'

'Wahey!'

'"She was given a chest as a wedding present. But there was a catch: Pandora was told she was not allowed to open it. This made her very curious about what was inside. Every time she saw it, she wanted to open it." (What do you think it might be?)'

'PS3.'

'Nah, nah, Xbox.'

'Yeah.'

'"Her heart was thumping.

'"Click. The key turned.

'"Clunk. The latch opened and fell to the floor.

'"BANG!"'

'Ah!'

'What?'

'Bang!'

'Blup, blup!'

'Man got bwuk up!'

'Is it? She get shot?'

Three SMs have been past my door in the last minute on their Learning Walks. The more they look in, the more tense I get. The more tense I get, the more I shout. Time for some directed questioning.

'So what kind of furniture does Pandora own? Anyone? Come on, we just read it.'

Come on, you cretins.

'A wardrobe? A chair? A table? Kieran? Any ideas. Any. Ideas. At. All.'

'Is it . . . umfing . . .?'

'No, Kieran, it is not *umfing*. Anyone want to read on? No? OK: "The lid of the CHEST burst open and Pandora was knocked to the ground by an icy, howling gale. Then the most disgusting, revolting, slimy things poured out of the chest." (What are the most disgusting things you can imagine? Don't answer that.) "Death. Disease. Poverty. Misery. Sadness. And at the bottom of the chest . . . Hope. Fluttering. Away . . ."'

Giggling, sliding down chairs, beating the desks with their arms.

An SM intervened.

'Be quiet! All of you! You, come here!'

Donnie was disappeared.

'"Prometheus could not help the mud-people. He dangled from the cliff, wriggling and writhing, but he could not break free of his chains. The universe was filled with the sound of crying."'

It had been a car-crash lesson. I had fundamentally failed to establish any authority. Quite the opposite: I had lost what precious little I had to begin with. And now it would take a Sisyphean effort to establish control.

The Year 8 Set 3s went the same way, and the Year 9 Set 2s. By the end of my lessons there were more kids outside the classroom than in, conspicuously filling up the corridors, dragging their pens up and down the putty between the giant panes of glass. Everyone who walked past could see I was a failure; this was compounded by the guilt I felt that I had now created so much more work for the SMs who would have to discipline the miscreants. I trudged disconsolately along the corridor.

HoD emerged from one of his lessons, with a throng of kids following him like the Pied Piper. When he stopped to speak to them, a tiny bunged-up boy looked up at him in awe and said, 'What. Teacher. Are. You?'

As I opened the door to the Department, the smell of BO knocked me backwards. A scrum of kids was waiting for the detentions I had given that day.

Lesson #5
Your Quality as a Teacher Is Inversely Proportional to the Number of Detentions You Give: the Better You Are, the Fewer Detentions You Give.

I had given most of the kids I had taught that day a detention; ergo, I was a shit teacher.

Little Miss Outstanding looked at me smugly; she had to give only three detentions.

Yeah, but you've got that piece-of-piss Set 2!

The other teachers gave me sympathetic or patronising smiles. It's very difficult to read teachers' faces. The experienced ones have become so adroit at hiding everything behind their composed carapace, the fixed grin is often meaningless. I struggled to my desk, and opened the twenty-five emails that had arrived during the lesson. Students missing from lessons; schemes of work for the year; plaintive attempts to swap duties; the PTA fun run; the Head of HR's pencil case was missing.

I had to get away from people. All I wanted to do was run out of the gates and not stop until I reached the sea, and breathe the fresh, hormoneless air gusting over the empty world.

A French NQT came in and collapsed on the seat next to me.

'Ah feel lahk ze whole world just came in my face,' she said.

Zackly, as the kids would say.

3

Go Toilet

'Can I go toilet?'

'Only if you ask properly.'

'Sir, can I go toilet?'

'You still haven't asked properly.'

'Sir, please can I go toilet! Sir, please?'

'That is still grammatically incorrect.'

Student looks baffled and confers with confidante.

'Is it that you want me to be more formal?'

'Yes, all right then. Why not be more "formal"?'

'Please, Mr Teacher, can I go toilet?'

'No, you still haven't got it.'

Student confers with confidante.

'Please, Secret, can I go toilet?'

'What?'

'That's your name, right? That's what it says on the school email. Secret Teacher.'

'Yes, but you're still not asking properly.'

'I am aksing proper.'

'Asking properly.'

'Zackly. Please, Your Highness Lord Mr Secret Teacher Your Most Excellency . . . Can I go toilet?'

'You're missing something crucial. Two things in fact: a preposition and the definite article.'

Student confers with confidante.

'Please, Your Highness Lord Mr Secret Teacher Your Most Excellency . . . The bell's about to go so you gotta let me go toilet.'

'No.'

'Allow it! I'm gonna go on the floor!'

'See? You can use the definite article!'

'Eh?'

'You can say "the"! You said "the floor"! So how do you ask to go toilet properly?'

'Can I go on the floor?'

'Same construction. Just not "the floor", but "the" . . . ?'

'Eh?'

'Where do you go toilet? I mean, where should you go? Not on *the* floor, but in . . .'

'Toilet.'

'*The* toilet. So what you meant to ask was . . . ?'

'Can I go – ?'

'*To* . . .'

'TO . . .'

'*The* . . .'

'THE . . .'

'Toilet.'

'Toilet.'

'So put it all together and what do you have?'

'OhpleasesirstopthisIswearIain'tlyingI'mgonnapee mypantiesjustlemme GO TO THE TOILET, Lord Sir Excellent Whatever.'

'Hallelujah.'

I had this conversation about five times a day.

4

Learning Walk

My beautiful Palace of Light had become an aquarium of angst. A Petri dish of pedagogic pain.

I was trapped in the Death Star. Stormtroopers were at my door all day long, zapping me, nuking me. I was brittle, impatient, fearful and strung out. Bare stressed, as the kids would say. I snapped and jumped down kids' throats, which only exacerbated their goading of me. They could sense my fear, as I sweated and loosened my collar.

The SMs could smell blood from the other side of the school. They swam, propelled by single beats of their tails, until they reached the coral in which the fat, feeble blowfish was stuck. They circled and prepared to attack, looking for any excuse – a head on a desk, a torso turned around, a giggle – whereupon the shark bared its teeth and tore chunks out of the child. And then a glare at me to acknowledge that chunks would come out of me later.

My Set 1s were fine; they just got on with whatever. My Year 8 Set 2s and my Year 9 Set 3s were still tricky, but at least they responded to the SMs, and most of them had parents you knew would give them both barrels when they got home. The Year 7 Set 4s didn't give a shit. It was like they had arrived from a distant planet on which consequences did not exist. They didn't have any notion of authority whatsoever, and didn't understand that these

SMs could do very bad things, like throw them out of school forever. There was little or no support from home, and without that, we were screwed. I'd try to call Kieran's mum and she'd say, 'Call his dad!' And then I'd call his dad, and he'd say, 'Call his mum!' Or they would try and turn it around and make it my fault.

Which of course it was.

Lesson #6
It's Always the Teacher's Fault.

All misbehaviour in the classroom, all academic failure, all failure of bodily functions, all failure of any kind is now the fault of the teacher.

VP was at the door of the Year 7 Set 4s the whole time, disappearing ne'er-do-wells. At the end of the lesson, I would come out, with my shirt untucked, tie askew, arms stacked with exercise books, still shouting at kids, squabbling with them as I walked down the corridor, passing the Jedi Knights with ten years' experience. I was the spluttering tugboat to their majestic galleons. VP would watch my entire walk of shame. As I turned to enter my next classroom, she would raise her eyebrow, pucker her mouth, turn on her heel, and go to talk to HoD.

After another of my nightmare lessons with the Year 7 Set 4s, HoD called me in and closed the door. On his desk was a Lesson Observation form, with 'Inadequate' highlighted repeatedly.

There's probably a P45 under that. I'm for it. I reckon I might not even make it past the end of the month.

'I've just been talking to VP.'

Sinking. Shades enveloping me. Down into the Underworld.

'She mentioned . . .' HoD caught a smirk and inhaled sharply.

'What?'

'Well. Something slightly sensitive.'

What? What have I done? I left something on my computer. Didn't I? My Facebook. Other websites I might have accidentally gone on late at night. Images of ghastly people doing ghastly things. Every memory I ever had. Projected in assembly. Head pointing at it with a red laser saying, 'This is an example of how not to live. This is not a role model. You must avoid this man at all costs!'

'You need to sort out your walk,' he said.

See? Told you. Take a walk. You're out of here.

'I knew it.'

'You did? I find that surprising. I wouldn't have guessed it in a million years. Fucking funniest thing I ever heard.'

'I'm glad you think it's funny. I don't. I thought I was just starting to get somewhere.'

'Clearly not. Clearly we have fundamental issues to iron out. Cause for Concern, I'd say.'

'Sorry, I don't understand. Am I being fired?'

'No, you bell-end,' said HoD. 'Your walk. Sort it out.'

'My walk? What's wrong with it?'

'It's too nonchalant.'

'Is it?'

'Yes.'

'Oh.'

'Let's have a look at it. Go on.'

'Go on: what?'

'Just walk to the door and back, would you?'

I gingerly stood up and walked to the door and back.

'Yeah, see. Far too laid back. You're nearly horizontal. You look like you're about to lay your towel down and sunbathe. You need some purpose. Dynamism. A bit of va-va-voom. Watch VP. Copy her.'

I went back to the Department and opened up my email. HoD had sent me an image of a walking leg, annotated to show all the key muscles. Sartorius. Vastus medialis. Tibialis anterior. Rectus femoris. Vastus lateralis. Gastrocnemius. Soleus.

VP strode past the window on an unwavering, inviolable mission. I was just about to practise walking to the coffee machine, when Little Miss Outstanding waltzed in, balancing sugar paper covered in spider diagrams and Post-its. She looked flushed. Everyone was all over her: 'Oh, well done you! Looks like such a great lesson! Can I borrow it?'

Pathetic.

Pathetic. Fallacy.

During the initial Terror, Little Miss Outstanding would run up to me after every lesson with the look of someone fleeing a besieged village. I would calm her down, and try to reassure her by telling her that, while the walls of our Death

49

Star garbage chute were closing in, R2D2 was going to work out how to disable the system any moment. Now it was clear Mentor was taking a shine to Little Miss Outstanding. She had thought the sun shone out of her SMARTboard since she had done a lesson on Pathetic Fallacy in *Macbeth*. 'Hubble bubble, storm and trouble' and all that. Guess what, kids? Bad weather is OMINOUS. It makes you think BAD THINGS ARE ABOUT TO HAPPEN. She got 'Outstanding' for that lesson, natch. I told her I was happy for her and she said it looks like R2D2 finally rescued us, and I said, 'Well, you at least. I'm still down the incredibly smelly garbage chute with the giant snake with the single eyeball dragging me under the sewage.' And then I covered one of her lessons and one of the kids – who was clearly not all there – said 'Innit sir you're mentally unstable? Dat's what Miss said.' She was actively undermining me to the kids! This was war.

She would come into the Department at lunchtime and say, 'Coming to lunch?' I would say, 'Sure', and we would walk across the playground together, and then just as I got close to the Canteen, I would bend down and tie up my shoelaces and tell her to go on ahead. Then I would sneak out of the side gate, walk to the manky Italian trattoria on the corner, order my toasted chicken escalope sandwich and take my greasy parcel to the graveyard. I sat there staring at the graves of Christians and Jews and Undecideds and think about the Montagues and Capulets, Pip and the convict, and all the people under my feet.

At least they're under control.

What a lesson this is.

I picked up the paper on a bench, hoping to numb myself with stories of the real world. But I had long lost contact with such a place.

Celebrities I have never heard of were not going out with each other.

House prices expensive.

Weather. Pathetic.

Oh, and an enormous machine gun has been found in the bushes of the estate next to the school.

Outside is violence and peril. Keep the outside out.

I went back to school to prepare for another Observation.

I got into teaching because I was attracted to its secrets. It is not like everything else: everything – everything in the world – that is now public, emetic, exposed. It's the last bastion of intimacy and integrity.

Teaching is a very private experience, whether you are teaching one or thirty children in a class. The teacher must establish a safe, impregnable dominion of trust within the classroom, in which the child feels protected, nurtured, understood, valued, and able to be themselves. This is a very delicate ecosystem, which is too easily disrupted. I'm not sure I ever really understood Vygotsky's Zone of Proximal Development, which you learn about in the first week of teacher training, but maybe that's what he was getting at. If it means 'a zone in which we can communicate and grow and learn from each other' then that's it. The classroom is a sacred space. When anyone comes in from the outside, it feels like an invasion of trust. Neither the teacher nor the kids behave the same way as they do when you are alone with them with the door shut. Everyone performs, and the entire process becomes a charade. To many teachers, Observations are a false economy and the bane of their lives; others recognise that they are a necessary evil. We have yet to find another way of monitoring teachers, and helping them to improve. To be is to be perceived.

I was on two or three Observations a week; some 'Formal', some 'Informal'. But we all knew there's no real difference. The SMs come in and informally and casually hang around for five minutes, and then informally and casually report back to the Imperial Forces that you are Inadequate and need a Formal Observation. It's like Book Checks. One minute they were 'Book Checks', the next 'Book Looks'. What's next? A Book Peek? A Book Glance Through One Eye? Doesn't matter how you try to downplay it, you're still invading my world.

Each Observation was with a teacher from a different discipline, who wanted something totally different from the last one. They basically had orders to make you feel like you were shit, but not so shit that you didn't have the confidence to teach. So you hover around the Inadequate/Requires Improvement borderline. Inadequate Man Requires Improvement.

I was getting marked down for tiny nothings – on 11 minutes, Mercedes looked at the clock; on 23 minutes Kieran did not seem to know what he was supposed to be doing; on 35 minutes Milosz had his hands down his pants; on 57 minutes Kieran didn't seem to know what he was doing.

Of course he didn't, Kieran never knows what he is doing! He has only just found the classroom for the first time, for Christ's sake! I should be getting Outstanding for the fact that they all managed to find the classroom before the lesson finished.

Lesson #7
Your Language Will Be Infected by OFSTED Jargon.

It doesn't matter that you are an English Teacher, a role model of erudition. Soon your language will be a Rattle-bag of OFSTED rubric. When Friday night rolls around, you will utter, 'That curry was Outstanding', or perhaps 'That curry was Required Improvement.' And one day you will say to a child, 'Your homework is Outstanding', and you will realise that it means it has yet to be done. It is extant. Like a parking ticket. Or a dream deferred.

After the Observation comes the dreaded Feedback session, which is all about the self-reflection.

How do *you* think it went?

I thought it was turd. Did you? Oh, good. Well, there we are. We are in agreement then. I am turd.

It's not about being perfect – every lesson is ragged in parts, you can never predict or control exactly how it is going to go – but a good observer knows that if the observed can work out what the problem was, then they can rectify it next time. If the observed simply shuts down and cannot take any criticism, then there is no hope of making any progress at all. It helps if the observer can be as self-deprecating as possible, and talk through all the mistakes they still make – because we all do, all the time.

Mentor would take me to a quiet classroom, shut the door with the deliberate solemnity of somebody closing the lid on a coffin and put her notes on the table (which I scanned for a judgement, but noticed that she had given up halfway through the lesson).

We were like disappointed post-coital lovers. She looked up at me, shrugging with resignation as I squirmed.

'How do you think it went?'

'Sorry.'

'It's OK. Don't worry about it. It happens to everyone.'

'I know. I just . . . really hoped that this time would be different.'

'It will get better. As long as we can identify where the problems are. And it wasn't all bad. There were lots of positives. Lots.'

'Did you really think so?'

'Oh, yes.'

'I'll nail it next time.'

It didn't help that my Mentor was the best teacher in the world ever. Every time I observed her I felt sick with envy. Like this one on Persephone and the Pomegranate Seeds.

The Starter was a brainstorm of tempting words (delicious, yummy, sticky); then she gave them a slice of pomegranate, and they had to fill in a grid to describe it, using the different senses; then she introduced examples of persuasive speech (AFOREST: Alliteration, Facts, Opinion, Repetition/Rhetorical Questions, Emotive Language, Statistics, Triples); then they had to spot the persuasive features in one of Obama's speeches; finally, they had to incorporate the features into their own persuasive speeches, which they then delivered. She was calm and authoritative throughout; she never shouted or lost her rag, because she never needed to.

Lesson #15
Engagement Is the Best Form
of Behaviour Management.

The kids felt nurtured, inspired, motivated and happy. The speeches were knockout. Even the most recalcitrant kids were giving expressive, excitable, almost articulate speeches, imploring us to eat the pomegranate ('Don't you wanna eat dis sticky, succulent, scrummy pomegranate? I know you do! Yeah you do! Did you know dat like 95 per cent of people in the Underworld said dey liked pomegranates? Go on! EAT IT, EAT IT, EAT IT!')

Amazeballs. They say you know Outstanding when you see it. It was going to take a fuckload of work.

I decided to teach that lesson.

Lesson #21
It Is Very Difficult to Teach
Other People's Lessons.

We all did it. When you've got five minutes to plan, you just nick one of VP's and change the font. But then you find yourself halfway through a lesson going, 'What the hell am I supposed to do now?'

It started well enough. I told them that if they were good and didn't call out or insult each other and kept their hands by the side of their desks and generally stayed still they could eat some pomegranate, which was actually even yummier and stickier and sweeter and juicier and more succulent than Haribos.

But everything went wrong as soon as I produced the pomegranate.

I didn't want to pass it round – definitely a recipe for disaster – so I walked around with it, letting them have a good look. 'Ugh, dat is butters!' shouted Mercedes, as I genuflected before her, offering the pomegranate in a spirit of submissive piety, the red, succulent, juicy flesh a millimetre from her nose. VP appeared. Perfect timing. I tried to play the Obama speech. The video wouldn't work.

Lesson #27

The Video Never Works.

When YouTube Finishes Buffering –

Finally! - An Inappropriate, Loud Pop-Up

Will Create Hilarity, Disruption.

They all became restless. Kieran offered to help. He approached the computer. Then, inevitably, he tried to put on a grime video, so I waved him away, and he sat down in a sulk. I told them to get on with describing the pomegranate, but they said they couldn't see it, so they gathered around the pomegranate and were trying to grab it and getting all sticky and messy. Suddenly, an explosion of violence from a computer game advert at top volume. They pissed themselves laughing, pink pomegranate juice dripping down their faces and shirts, as VP entered the classroom. Donnie and Mercedes were told to go to the toilet and clean themselves up. Slowly, the rest returned to their seats.

The Obama speech proved entrancing, so I followed the YouTube recommendations and put on a video of one of Churchill's speeches after the Obama speech. When I said, 'Who is that?', no one knew. Kieran said, 'What, the dog?' Everyone fell about. Donnie and Mercedes returned from the bathroom as the bell went.

After the lesson, I cleaned up the sticky pink mess that was all over the desks. Mentor stuck her head in.

'Can I have a word?'

'Sure.'

'What was going on in that lesson?'

'I tried to teach your pomegranate lesson and it went pear-shaped.'

'Bad luck.'

'What did VP say?'

'Not much.'

'Formal Observation?'

'Yup.'

The thing that really screws you with Observations is the marking. Every book has to be bang up to date, and when you have 120 books to mark a week, a few are bound to fall through the cracks. I spent so much time chasing kids for books. Every lesson I asked for them, and every lesson they forgot them.

I thought about walking around the estate, smeared in mud, dressed in a chaperon hood, banging a saucepan, dragging a cart full of exercise books, shouting, 'Bring out your English books!' (If you want to give them up anonymously, you can leave them in the big metal bin full of knives.)

The Set 1s were the worst. Not because they didn't do the work, but because they did. Absolutely filled the pages. Couldn't stop. Redid work, did extra; extension task to the extension tasks. Ten pages a homework. Tick. Tick. Tick. Level 7. Congratulations! Another fabulous story! Target: CALM DOWN. You're ELEVEN YEARS OLD.

It was six o'clock on Friday and I still had all my books to mark from the week. There was no way I would usually work on a Friday night, but there was a Book Look on Monday. (First Prize: dinner for two at ASK Pizza; free tiramisu for a book with red or green pen on every page.) Tom had already marked all his books – he reckoned he had got it down to two minutes per book, the flash git – while I had done five in half an hour. Tom bundled out, saying, 'See you in the Library!' I couldn't be arsed to mark; I was so tired; the handwriting was illegible; I could barely read any of the work; what I could read was dog shit. I sat there listening to the dripping coffee machine, daydreaming about a passionate embrace under a water-fall, when an email pinged.

An Invitation to a Formal Observation
with VP.
Friday, Period 8, Rm 11. Year 7 Set 4.

Fuck. She knew that's when the little bastards would be at their most feral. She could have come in Monday, Period 1, when they were totally lobotomised after a weekend of Grand Theft Auto. But no. She had to come when they would be bouncing off the walls.

I put my head on the pile of books. HoD patted me on the shoulder. 'Time for the Library.'

5

The Library

It's not really a library. Most teachers wouldn't be caught dead in a real library. They just like to talk about going to the pub in front of kids and feel the illicit thrill of espionage. But the kids know the score.

Around 4 p.m., the kids charged around the corner, demob happy – tie around forehead, rucksack around neck – to be confronted by most of their teachers milling around outside the pub, laughing, flirting, rolling rollies and downing pints. The kids smirked, then dived behind cars in order to spy on us. They assumed that if they saw you having a drink with another teacher then you must be going out with them, so on Monday morning one of your class would pipe up, 'I saw you in the pub with Miss on Friday!' And the rest of the class would go 'Oooooooo-hhhhhhh! Was you gettin' WAVY?'

I struggled through the double doors with my three tote bags full of exercise books. HoD handed me a pint and shouted, 'Come sing me a bawdy song and be merry!' He was clearly steaming.

'Get that jumper off. Just chuck it in the bin. Drink that. There. You deserve it. Now. Who the fuck do you think you are, anyway?'

I attempted to remove my jumper, which crackled with static as it passed over my head, and pushed the tote bags under the table. Tom moved his bag out of the way, so I could sit, and put his arm round my shoulder.

'Honestly,' continued HoD. 'Rocking up here. Walking into a room full of kids and expecting them to listen to you. Who do you think you are?'

He tore a packet of roasted peanuts down the middle and poured them into his mouth.

'Why do you want to teach?' he asked, spitting peanuts on my shoes.

'Er . . . because I want to make a difference.'

'Oh God, no. Please no. Anything but that.'

'Oh, OK. Sorry, because I love my subject –'

'Oh God, no. Please no. Anything but that.'

'Oh, OK. Because I hate my subject.'

'That's more like it.'

He was momentarily distracted by Paula, the Teaching Assistant, who walked past. He planted a big squelchy kiss on her cheek, saying, 'Y'alright, darlin'?'

'Why do *you* teach?' I asked.

He laughed a deep, guttural laugh.

'What else is there?'

'Right. Zackly,' I said.

'Nuff said. Right? Am I right?'

I nodded. Even when it was terrible – which it was right now – there was nothing else I wanted to be doing.

'Teaching is the nuts. Always was, always will be. You've been around the block. You've seen the vacuous dead world outside. And then you enter the classroom . . . and it's just . . . Life! Curiosity! Learning! Laughter! Joy! Once you've been in that room, you can't do anything else. I don't care where. I could teach anywhere. Just give me a room, some kids, a book. Nothing like it.'

He threw the empty nut packet on the table and slapped his leg in appreciation.

'But it's changing so fast. I'm already a dinosaur. I don't know if I can take it much longer. Look around you. See anyone over thirty? No, me neither. There's a philosophy here. Get 'em young, burn 'em out, ship 'em off. You all have a three-year shelf life. Max. You're just collateral. Utterly replaceable. I mean, teachers are just trouble after a few years, aren't they? They get demanding and up themselves and stuck in their ways and sloppy and pregnant and change their priorities and lose focus and ill and dead and all that inconvenient crap. I mean look at this guy.'

He pointed to a fat elderly gentleman perched on a stool. Apparently, he had once been an SM, but I only knew him as the guy who drove the minibus.

'This guy has been here since the dawn of time. You should see his Assembly on the Blitz. Eyewitness stuff. The kids have got their eyes on stalks when he tells them what he's seen. He's seen it all. Haven't ya? It's not changed a bit, has it?'

The old gent snorted.

'Ah, the good old days, eh?' HoD continued. 'Don't believe what you hear. It used to be great. No uniforms. No sets. Not much discipline. Yeah, it was rough round the edges. Kids from everywhere. From the local estate, the liberal middle classes, then the riffraff from the wrong side of the river. I'm not saying there wasn't tension. You get all these local intellectuals and grandees who worry about the ruffians frightening away the nightingales. But we basically muddled along. Ah, it was magic.'

He drained his pint.

'Now all I do is fill in crap just so there is some evidence that we are doing stuff. I should be having a conversation with you about that last shit lesson you taught and we should be filling this out.'

He waved my Lesson Evaluation contemptuously in front of my nose.

'But you only saw the first and last minute.'

'That's enough for me. I'm right though, aren't I? It was total arseshit. But it's not important what I think. How do *you* think it went?'

'Pretty shockingly.'

'Good. No arguments there. What would you do differently?'

'Everything.'

'Anything in particular?'

'Less Chalk and Talk.'

'*Boom ting*. Once upon a time, you could have got away with a lesson like that. In the old days, if you could charm them, that was enough. The Old Head would come round and as long as they weren't swinging from the chandeliers, he would walk on. We would just read and talk. About anything. Fuckin' *quality*. Can you identify when you lost control?'

'Beginning.'

'There you go. Get on top of them in the first five minutes, it will be fine. Lose them, and you will be chasing them around for the whole hour. Like a cat chasing a tissue in the breeze. And so it goes.'

He scrawled a couple of words and his signature and handed the crumpled form back to me.

'Look, I'll be honest,' I wheezed, as the warm glow from the ale spread across my throat and lungs, 'I've been really struggling. I mean, everywhere I look I see amazing teachers doing amazing things. And I can't even get past first base. I can't control the kids. They don't respect me. I don't see a way out.'

HoD nodded. 'Don't be intimidated by all the whizz-bangery, OK? I don't do any of that shit. Look, it's all about doing just enough to keep the SMs away from your door.'

I struggled to put the form back in my unwieldy Progress Record folder.

'I thought it was all about instilling a love of learning. I thought it was all about the kids.'

'Good God, man, where did they find you? Summerhill? Look: you have to play the game. Would it be possible to do this job without this entire raft of bollocks? Of course it would. But they –'

He gestured wildly with his arm towards a region around his head.

'*They* don't understand that. *They* think they have reached Shangri-La *on* the raft of bollocks. As long as we all believe the raft of bollocks is the only route, you've got to get on board.'

I looked nervously around me.

'Don't worry. You won't see them down here. Once upon a time, the whole lot of us would come down here on a Friday. It was mental. Just having a proper session and a right laugh. We used to have staff meetings down here. Now you won't find a single one of those autobots down here. They're not allowed. It's seen to be unprofessional. Doesn't fit the corporate ethos. They're up there all night – they'll be there all weekend filling in data, I guarantee it.'

He reached over and took another pint from Tom's tray with a wink.

'Stop stressing. Chill out. It's all about teaching between the cracks. You find these precious cracks between the great monoliths of assessment and observation and OFSTED and the exam boards and every bloody other thing that is not about you there in that room with those kids imparting wisdom. Just give me a room and some kids. Seriously. That's all I need. Once I shut the door, I shut it all out. And they love it. I give them time to reflect, look out of the window, get lost in a sunbeam, like Keats. Not much chance of any Negative Capability with all your gubbins flying around.'

'Are you suggesting that for my Observation with Year 7 Set 4, I just say, "Look at this sunbeam"?'

'No. You'll get eaten alive. But understand that you will reach a stage where you can do less. And less, my friend, is most definitely more.'

'That's right,' said Tom. 'Watch this guy. You will definitely see less.'

'Yeah, all right,' replied HoD, testily. 'I don't do much with them. But, boy, do they work for me.'

'That they do. I don't know how you do it,' replied Tom.

'"The days that make us happy make us wise." We have fun. They think reading is rebellious, which it is. Not necessarily the book we have to do. But the books I recommend they read on the sly at the end of the lesson, at break time, on the walk home. You are beginning a series of relationships. And relationships take time. I can see a good teacher within five minutes. You'll win 'em round soon, the fuckers will peel away, and then you'll be in clover.'

Ho6 burst through the doors in tears, and was soon enveloped in HoD's bear embrace.

'All right, love. Come here. What happened? Are they being beastly to you again?'

She nodded and drank fast as she wiped away her tears. She had just been observed for the umpteenth time that week with her Year 11s. The SMs were after her since her GCSE English Language results. Her Set 1s were predicted A*s and As, but were awarded Ds and Es. The SMs has told her they were going to come into her lessons for an indefinite period. They wouldn't tell her which lessons. Every lesson would have to be 'Outstanding'. It takes forever to plan and mark for an 'Outstanding' lesson; she would have to spend all weekend planning and marking and stressing.

'Don't worry. We've appealed about the results,' said HoD as he handed her a pint.

'Fuckers,' she said. 'I've been teaching since before they were at Accenture or Orange or wherever the hell it was. I had a meeting at 6 a.m. this morning about the appropriate length of girls' skirts or some bollocks. I was just sat there looking up at them, and I couldn't hear a word they were saying. All I could see were the annotated verses from *Paradise Lost* my Year 13s had stuck to the wall, and I imagined I was Satan plotting my rebellion against God.'

Tom told me to drink up. He had invited me to a dinner party with some friends of his. 'Izzit dough,' I said. I was flatlining teacher drunk: helpless, in desperate need of direction, capable only of uttering phrases used by kids: 'izzit dough'; 'bare jokes'; 'gotta go toilet'.

Lesson #51

When Not Speaking in OFSTED Jargon,
You Will Speak Like Your Pupils.

Somehow, armed only with this vocabulary, I was going to have to navigate a posho dinner party.

Tom and I staggered out of the pub into the cold dark night and weaved along the road.

The next thing I remember was walking into a plush second-floor flat. My first thought was 'Yikes, Grown-ups!' The guys were all chiselled and floppy-haired and wearing suits – not like M&S teacher suits, but proper Gieves & Hawkes numbers – while their wives were in elegant dresses. They stood with wine glasses in one hand, and ate canapés with the remaining hand, having adult, braying conversations.

When did my generation start behaving like this? Was there an INSET day I missed?

The men seemed very uncomfortable with me, which was partly because I was so drunk, but also because I had not been to school or university with them, so they couldn't place me. The host came over and patted me on the shoulder.

'Mate, mate, how's it going, basically?'

'I'm fine,' I lied.

'Mate, were you at Edinburgh?'

'No. No, I wasn't.'

'Sure? You look familiar.'

'No. Somewhere else.'

We stared at the floor. I thought he was going to move away, but he was determined to stoke the dying embers of our bantz.

'Nice. Nice. So, er . . . how do you know Tom?'

'Um . . . teaching?'

'Oh, yah, great. Great stuff. Must be so rewarding.'

'Mmmm.'

'Nice holidays.'

'Mmmm.'

'Skiing.'

'Mmmm.'

'Have you met Gus? He's a teacher too. Not sure where. Somewhere bit dodgy. Loves it though. Keep trying to get him to cash in his chips and come back to the dark side, but he's sticking with it. Couldn't do it myself. Thought about teaching. But then I thought how much I hated my teachers. Reckon I might be rotten at it too.'

'Mmmm.'

I heard someone say something about 'pupillages'. 'I have pupils!' I interjected with gauche violence. Everyone stared at me as if a cow were mooing in the corner of the room. I stood in a fug, staring at the floor, grasping at the mantel-piece. A wave of nausea started to roll up from my belly. I muttered 'Gotta go toilet' and lurched towards the bathroom.

After the last empty retch, I stared at myself in the chrome pan. Even here, I was observed.

When I came out of the bathroom, and gingerly sat down at the dinner table, I composed myself, and flicked the napkin across my lap, staring at the milky white liquid in the bowl in front of me. I felt another heave from below.

'Vichyssoise,' said the host, with mock-oleaginous relish, which failed to disguise the fact that this was actually how he spoke.

The tall, glossy, blond woman next to me introduced herself as something imposing. She told me she was a barrister. I told her about the Year 9 lesson I taught that day in which I asked what they wanted to be when they grow up, and a boy told me he wanted to be a 'bannister'.

'How charming. It's a state school, I take it?'

'Yes. How did you know?'

'Golly. Well done you. Do they come from all over?'

'Yes. All over. *Everywhere.*'

I made a large globe with my arms, knocking my wine glass over as I did so.

'It must be very challenging teaching all these different types of children.'

'Yes. Yes, it is. But there are lots of different ways of doing it.'

'Oh. Like what?'

'Oh, you know . . .'

I shrugged, and stuffed a soggy brown roll into my mouth.

'Must be so rewarding,' she said.

'Hmm. Must be. Haven't got to that bit yet.'

'Nice holidays.'

'Mmmm.'

'I had a teacher once . . .'

Lesson #60

Everyone wants to talk about education.
And they all think schools should be
like the one they went to. Or the
diametric opposite.

The next thing I remember, Tom was shaking me awake. As I woke, I lurched up from the table and groaned something about having to get photocopies.

A vague recollection of the streaked blue lights on the windscreen; shock-jock babble on the radio; an exchange of money with a man who may or may not have been a cab driver.

I woke at 4 a.m. on the sofa, my mouth lined with furry mould. I leapt up, thinking I was late for school, then realised with unalloyed joy that it was Saturday. *Saturday! Saturday! Saturday, it's Saturday!* After my celebratory dance around the house, I stumbled into the bedroom and watched Amy sleeping. She looked so beautiful and peaceful. I couldn't remember the last time we ate together, or went out, or talked. Or . . .

She's taught me so much. How to love. How to live. How to turn the back windscreen wiper off.

'You stink. Go and sleep in the spare room.'

That's nice, that is.

I stared at the wall in the spare room. Alone at last. No

kids, no teachers, no emails.

There is officially nothing in my brain. I have successfully unwound myself so that I see the world like a Year 7 Set 4.

Ah! There they are again, little bastards! Invading my nether conscious like incubi – floating, dancing, taunting. Mercedes growling, Kieran cackling, Milosz sliding under his chair. Fuck off!

Thank you.

Maybe I'll just check my emails.
    Just a quick check of Rate My Teacher.
    No. Don't. Seriously.
    Just a peep.
    Oh God. One stars across the board.
    Someone must have something good to say.
    Mercedes. I love you.
    I am a failure.

So self-indulgent. They have problems. They have real issues. And you think it's all about yourself? All is vanity.

What Teacher Are You?

Why am I doing this shit job? All I do is Plan, Mark, Deliver. Plan, Mark, Deliver. When did teaching become 'delivery'? Am I an Amazon drone? That's the future. Right there. How many stars would you give Mr Teacher? Those who bought Mr Teacher's lessons, also bought: *Hamlet*. Montaigne's essays. David Foster Wallace. A gun.

I am so tired. This is what they meant when they said the NQT was one of the most gruelling programmes around. Up there with Sandhurst, the Chinese Civil Service, Iron Man and NASA.

So peaceful.

Apparently, the only job where you have more human interactions than teaching is air-traffic controller.

Could do that.

Come into land.

Now take off.

At least my colleagues won't be eleven and insane.

I bet they are.

Cancel the holiday to Thailand.

Fucking Formal Obs with VP next week.

Fucknuts. Maybe I'll do some marking now.

Fuck! The books! I left the fucking books in the Library!

6

Painful Observation

THE SATURDAY BEFORE FORMAL OBSERVATION WITH VP

Pure unadulterated panic. Ran to the Library to try to find books. Not there. Rushed over to Tom's friend's house. 'Mate, how you feeling? Things got pretty messy? Quality,' he said. He didn't have my books. Called cab company. Not there.

SUNDAY

Watched hours of football, curled up in tense ball on the sofa. Googled 'Air Traffic Controller Training'. Argument with Amy about chronic lassitude. At least there weren't books all over the kitchen table for once.

MONDAY

Kept head down. Got all classes to write on paper. Avoided SMs all day. Managed to avoid Book Look. Resigned to not winning tiramisu. Just as I was about to slope off, Paula the TA came in with my bags of books. I hugged her tight, then smuggled the books home. God, I love Paula.

I covered the kitchen table with books. They had to be bang up to date. If there was a week's homework missing, or any work that was less than half a page, or if there was a single page without a green pen on it – mostly mine, but some of theirs to show Peer Assessment – I was dead.

There's nothing here. Nothing at all.

Try to chop vegetables while marking. Blood on white pages like snow after the savage bludgeoning of a seal pup.

Red marks. Smear the blood into a tick. Might get free tiramisu after all.

Oh God. There's nothing here. Nothing!

I desperately searched back to the beginning of term. Just half-pages of doodles and scrawl. A page with the title and a date and then nothing, a few empty pages, and then another title and date and nothing. A few lines. Then nothing.

MILOSZ'S BOOK

September 12th

MY GOD

My God is called XMAN and he is a badman u
don't wanna mess wiv bruv or mandems gonna
comeden and give you beatdowns

KIERAN'S BOOK

17th September

PUNDA'S BOX

Punda's Box is a box it is not like an Xbox it has all
the bad things innit you should not open it if you
do then bare bad things happen

Wot u lookin at fam

U R MOIST

A doodle of a man hanging.

Me.

That's me.

I ran all round the school trying to track them down. Form Time, Break, Lunch. Most were absent. Finally, I found Kieran drifting downstream.

'Kieran! Kieran! Is this your aptual – sorry, actual – book?'

(He had written 'aptual' once and now that was what I said. My mind and his were one.)

'Yeah.'

'I mean, you don't have another one somewhere?'

'No.'

'*This* is it? *This* is all you have done all year?'

'Fink so.'

Fuck.

I went through the books and marked the shit out of them. I ticked everything, gave constructive notes to the tiniest fragment. If there was half a sentence ('This shows that Pandora is curious!!!'), I gushed: *Stunning, Salim! Just try to use fewer exclamation marks!*

If it was at least half a page, I could give it a level. I even tried to fake their handwriting and write to the bottom of the page. I started giving levels to three sentences.

Kieran's is a disgrace.

This book is a disgrace.

Mother, welcome back.

THE LAST LESSON BEFORE THE FORMAL OBSERVATION
WITH VP

I gave their books back. When I gave Kieran's back, I told him I might as well throw it in the bin. He said, 'Go on den.' So I did. He didn't care.

It was time for the Pre-Observation Pep Talk.

'OK, everybody, quiet, please. Quiet. That means no talking. I'll wait. I can wait . . . Thank you. So next lesson we are having a very special visitor. The Vice Principal will be here.'

Ooohs and *aaah*s and *woopdadoo*s.

'OK, calm down. I know, exciting, isn't it?'

'Why?' Kieran shouted.

'Don't shout out, Kieran. Hands up.'

Kieran put his hand up.

'Why's she comin' in?'

'Because she wants to see you. Because I have told her how good you all are.'

'But we're not good.'

'Yes, you are.'

'No, we're not. You always tell us we're bad.'

He's got you there. Call yourself a teacher? All their bad behaviour, all their failings, are because of *your* failure to be constructive. All they ever wanted was a bit of love. You are a bad, bad man.

'I don't say that!'

'You do!' they shouted.

'Well, I apologise. You are not bad. Not all the time. Sometimes you are very good. Like now. Now you are being very good. So let's keep it this way, shall we? We'll do a deal: you be good to me, and I'll be good to you.'

'Deal!'

'Excellent. Next lesson I want you to make an extra-special effort to be *extra-specially* well behaved and to get on with your work as quickly as you can. And because it is an extra-special lesson, we are going to have an extra-special treat.'

'Haribos?'

'No. Group work.'

'Oh.'

'But you have to stay extra-specially focused throughout the group work, OK? You have to have your listening ears on. We have to work on our teamwork. We can't have a repeat of last time, can we, Kieran?'

'No, Sir.'

'No, Sir. That's right.'

'Now I've been looking at your books and I was not very happy with what I saw. No, I wasn't, Mercedes. Why would that be?'

Because you are your mother.

'Dunno.'

'Don't know, *Sir*. No. Well, you should. Most of them were missing masses of work. I have identified things I want you to redo for the rest of the lesson.'

For the last part of the lesson, I let them Peer Assess. Nothing turns SM on more than a bit of Peer Ass.

As a result of their inability to sit next to each other

without some kind of contretemps, I had changed the seating plan after each lesson, so that one by one they had been picked off until I was staring at a room of singles at paired seats. It was like looking at line of misfits at a bar, all of whom had been stood up, like the Edward Hopper painting *Nighthawks*.

(We used that for a creative writing exercise. They loved to imagine the backstory.

What happened that night?

Who are these lonely souls?

Write their dialogue.

Only use short words and sentences. Like the American short-story writers.

Write truth. On a Post-it.

What else is there?)

I created an elaborate book-ferrying system so they could mark each other's work. By the end of the lesson, they had redone work they couldn't remember doing, correcting the mistakes I had identified but making a whole raft of new ones, and had written some illegible critique of each other's work in massive green felt-tip, which tended to amount to *ad hominem* attacks on the person who happened to be closest to them.

YOUR WORK IS MOIST
LOW IT FAM

VP was going to lap it up.

I let them go. As Kieran was leaving, I took him to one side.

'Kieran, can I have a word, please?'

I handed him a new exercise book and told him that if VP asked to see his book, he had to pretend that he had lost it, and I had just given him this new one. He stared at me vacantly. I suggested we practise. He grunted his assent.

'OK. Kieran, why is there no work in your book?' I asked.

'We don't do nuffing in class.'

'No, that's not why, Kieran, is it? That's not true –'

'Yeah, it is.'

'No, you say you *lost your book*.'

You little shitass.

'I lost my book.'

'OK. And what were you doing last lesson?'

'Can't remember.'

I'll remember this, Kieran, when I'm rotting in the gulag.

THE NIGHT BEFORE MY FORMAL OBSERVATION
WITH VP

5 p.m. It had been hanging over me all week, but now, finally, after the last lesson of the day, the last detention, the last Parental Meeting, I could finally get down to it.

Think Pure Pedagogy.

Peda Goggy.

Peda Doggy.

Walk the Dog.

I jotted some ideas on a piece of paper.

What do I want them to do? Well, let's see, I want them to write a PEE paragraph about Echo and Narcissus. PEE. Three letters to make every NQT shudder. Other than NQT.

Point. Evidence. Explanation. Point: Narcissus loves himself. Evidence: We can see this in the line 'He was very vain.' Explanation: This shows that Narcissus is arrogant. He only looks at himself and does not care about anything around him (*extend explanation, tick, tick*).

Boom ting.

I looked on the system, and there were some lovely, clear lessons, well differentiated, that all the kids could access, like the one by VP.

But it looked so *boring*. I couldn't just trot out the same old lesson that everyone used, the one that VP had created, when I was being observed by VP. It had to be whizzy, right? All Singing All Dancing: cancan girls, grass skirts, hula hoops, margaritas, party hats. So I jazzed it up, and threw in lots of gubbins like Role Plays and Market Place Activities, clipboards, laminated role-play cards, dancing penguins. I cut out the faces of everyone in the class and stuck them on a slide and gave them all personalised, differentiated challenges covered with boxes that dissolved when you clicked on them.

Mercedes: Word Wizard! Note Down All The Key Words That You Hear In This Lesson! EXTENSION: Can You Use Them In A Sentence?

And then I saw it. A glistening mirage.

I could create *a lake*.

I could get lots of laminated cards with questions on them about Narcissus, and in their groups they would have fifteen minutes to ask each other those questions, and for each question they got right, they could turn over the card. And then when all of the cards had been turned over, the silver on the other side of the card would create an enormous reflective lake! And then – *oh, wow, here's the kicker* – then, when you looked in the lake, you would see *yourself*, as if in a mirror! And... And! If you squinted really carefully you could see on the ceiling of the classroom a Post-it with an Extension Task, like, say, 'Who Am I?' And the weakest could say, 'I'm Me'; the more able could say, 'I am Narcissus'; the slightly more able could say, 'I am Narcissus and I am in love with myself'; and the most able could say, 'I am a narcissist'; and the *most most* able could perhaps go into an existential digression about whether they are really who they are or merely a fictional construct. A reflection in the Lacanian mirror.

And then – and then, the *coup de grâce* – for the Plenary ... For. The. Plenary. We all sit round the lake and have a picnic! Yes. And have cake. And ask the person to our left what they have learned this lesson.

In party hats.

Oh, wow. *Oh, wow*. Oh. Wow. If I could pull this off... I mean we are talking, what? They would have to create a whole new category. Beyond Outstanding. She would have to say, 'This lesson was Outstanding with Exceptional features . . . No, scratch that. This lesson was Sublime with Beautiful Features. It was Kant's definition of the Noble Sublime: Absolutely Great. This lesson was, like the Buddhist Nirvana, Ineffable, and therefore beyond the realm of mortal language. I can only quote Wittgenstein: "Whereof one cannot speak, thereof one should be silent."'

5.48 p.m. I just had time to print off the resources before I went home. I shut down the computer and pushed my chair back, hastily pulling on my suit jacket. The screen reverted to the school logo.

Fuck. I didn't save. The whole fucking thing. The orange Trebuchet. The black background. The dancing penguins. All their faces. Disappeared.

I crumpled on the desk and wept.

Head of HR came in.

'Are you OK?' he said.

'Yes, fine.'

'Tough job,' he said. 'I totally understand. If you need anyone to speak to . . .'

'Thank you. Any sign of your pencil case?'

'No. No! NO! Can you believe it?' he shouted, storming out.

I exhaled violently and turned the computer back on. I ploughed on, emulating Carlyle rewriting his *History of the French Revolution* after he lost the first draft in a fire.

6.17 p.m. Little Miss Outstanding swanned in.

'Hi. How's it going?'

Don't talk to me. 'Fine.'

'Working on your Observation?'

'Yeah. Yeah. Just tweaking it now.'

'Is that with VP? The one you had to redo because you were Inadequate?'

How does she know that? HOW. DOES. SHE. KNOW. THAT?

'That's the one.'

'Do you want me to have a look?'

'I'm fine, thanks.'

'I can give you some pointers if you like. I think I know what she likes. She came to see me last week.'

Oh, I bet you know what she likes. I bet she came to see you and you were very accommodating.

'Just make sure it's tight,' she said.

'I'll try. Did you do much Peer Ass?'

'Yup. Paired work, group work, then individual. Visual, Aural, Kinaesthetic. We did a lollypop AFL Plenary that I was worried about, but I licked it. It was a dream.'

Oh God, you're making me sick. Let me guess: Pathetic Fallacy in subordinate clauses? And no, you don't need to tell me what you got. You reek of Outstanding.

She told me to sleep on it and that I should look at it fresh in the morning.

Easy for you to say, Little Miss Outstanding with Out-standing Features. Just go to Zumba already.

I tweaked. And tweaked. And tweaked.

I've totally fucked this up. This is going to be such a car crash.

2.14 a.m. I couldn't sleep.

There's so much that can go wrong with this lesson. I've got to get on top of them early. Anything, the slightest hint of the slightest mutter, they're straight out. But what if none of them get the Starter? I mean, maybe none of them know what vanity means? Mercedes is going to say something rude, then everyone will be in hysterics and I'll spend the whole lesson trying to regain control. Just don't let her speak. Must remember muzzle.

THE DAY OF MY FORMAL OBSERVATION WITH VP

5 a.m. I looked at the lesson on my laptop while I ate cereal. It didn't make any sense whatsoever.

6.06 a.m. Bought three packs of Haribos and some tin foil from Bananaman. He looked concerned.

6.36 a.m. Couldn't get into classroom, so had to finish it off in the atrium. Still had to write Lesson Plan.

Fuck, Lesson Plan!

I hastily wrote my Lesson Plan then tried to print it off, but there was a paper jam, so I printed it off on a printer that was located on the other side of the school. I ran across the playground, up the stairs. Wrong room. No printer. I finally found it tucked away in a DT Lab. I couldn't get in, and ran around frantically until I found a technician with a key. Nine pages had come out all streaky and garbled. I spent another ten minutes trying to work out how to print it two-sided.

Fuck Lesson Plan.

7.14 a.m. I still had to photocopy the resources, so I ran down to the photocopier, but there was an enormous queue of people photocopying their lessons for the whole day.

Honestly. It's not like any of them have Observations on Which Their Lives Depend. They're just printing off exam booklets for BTEC Social Sciences. Who gives a shit?

I remembered that Little Miss Outstanding always used coloured paper, and she was Outstanding, after all. Nothing wows SMs more, or says 'Learning Is Taking Place Here', than the old multi-coloured card.

Card's stuck. Shit! Shit!

'Bill! Sorry, can you . . . How about that game last night . . . sorry, it's not coming out . . . thanks!'

I had three minutes to guillotine and laminate.

Ah! Not again! What's wrong with this?

A Maths teacher came in and said, 'Observation?' And I said, 'How did you know?'

'You're having a Laminator Moment.'

'I didn't realise that was a Thing.'

'The only people who ever laminate are being observed.'

The card came out of the laminator all lumpy.

Honestly. What am I doing? I'm a teacher not a fucking *Blue Peter* presenter. Why can't I just go in there and read the book? I'll show you vanity. This! This is vanity! All is vanity.

FRIDAY, PERIOD 1

Nobody did any work on a Friday. The whole Department just sat there eating Cheese Strings, watching me sweat over my lesson. HoD told me to put a Cheese String Challenge into my lesson. I told him to fuck off.

FRIDAY, PERIOD 2

Year 8. Gave books back. They complained that they hadn't been marked. Told them to Peer Ass, then write about 'A Mysterious Parcel' while I tweaked my lesson.

FRIDAY, PERIOD 3

Year 9. Gave books back. They complained that they hadn't been marked. Told them to Peer Ass, then write about 'A Magical Journey' while I tweaked my lesson.

```
             Lesson #74
   You Will Not Teach Any Other Lessons
   Properly on the Day of an Observation.
      Your Classes Must Just Get On with
   Something, Anything, While You Obsess over
   Your Monumental Work. Like William Golding
   'Teaching' While Writing His Novels. Or Any
           of Those Old-School Cats.
```

FRIDAY LUNCHTIME

Pleading emails abounded.

```
From: The Secret Teacher
To: All Staff
Does anyone have a computer room P8?
  Please help!!!!!
  Please, please help.
```

PS Hope to see you in the Library this afternoon.

Then:

All Staff: Yeti is missing from Geography in Rm 10.

I tried to prepare the classroom during lunch break, but there was a boy praying on the floor.

And he only has one god! I have to teach all of them!

FRIDAY, PERIOD 7

Anyone with any experience or sense has booked a computer room. Room after room of deadened souls, headphones on, zoned out from the world and each other, working on something face-clawingly dull.

I went through the timings in my head, checking my props and rehearsing my lines. Fifteen-slide lesson, check; clipboards, check; large clump of scrunched foil with laminated buboes, check; nine-page Lesson Plan, check.

FIVE MINUTES BEFORE FORMAL OBSERVATION WITH VP

Need the toilet. Rush downstairs. Fuck. MegaDumper from ICT is in there! How dare he! They've got a toilet outside their Department! And there isn't another toilet for miles!

Oh God. What does he eat?

FRIDAY, PERIOD 8: MY FORMAL OBSERVATION WITH VP

A catastrophe. Everything went tits up.

They didn't understand nuffing. Not vanity, not Narcissus, not nada. They were drowning in a silver sea, adrift in the middle of the buboed foil, looking for guidance from me – the pathetic milquetoast, exhorting them to have fun and express themselves – then to VP – the terrifying Mrs Trunchbull who could make them sit down and shut up with a flicker of her eyes.

TEN MINUTES BEFORE THE END OF FORMAL OBSERVATION WITH VP

They've not completed any work. No manifest learning has taken place. I've just got to skip to the Plenary.

We sat around a scrunched-up, buboed lake in party hats, as a series of adverts for washing powder played on YouTube.

What have we learned?

Donnie?

Mercedes?

Three things we have learned this lesson.

Three things.

One thing we have learned this lesson.

One thing.

The Post-it fell off the ceiling.

FRIDAY, PERIOD 9: MY FEEDBACK WITH VP

I sat on the nice chair and tried to break the ice.

'Nice chair.'

She smiled. 'How do you think it went?'

Self-reflection. I am staring at my own reflection in buboed foil.

'Um . . . not great.'

She went through the lesson in detail.

'Starter – all distracted, chaotic beginning; main task – no one knew what they were doing, chaotic . . .'

Yeah, yeah. Just give it to me straight. I know it was Inadequate. Look, I'm being self-reflective. Can I get some extra points for that?

I knew what the problem was. Knew it the moment I started planning the damn thing.

Lesson #82
Don't Pitch It Above Their Heads. Go Low
And Then You Can Move Up Through The Gears
Once They Are With You. Don't Do What You
Think Is Whizzy and Cool. Do What They Can
Access and Understand.

After she went through all the problems, she said that she was impressed with my marking. She gave me Inadequate with Requires Improvement Features.

FRIDAY, PERIOD 9.5

I went back to the Department and dunked a teabag repetitively into a polystyrene cup.

Inadequate with Requires Improvement Features!

Now to aim for Requires Improvement with Inadequate Features. Or Outstanding with Inadequate Features. Or Inadequate with Outstanding Features. That's the moonshot, right there.

I opened up my email.

```
All Staff: Milosz thrown out of Oracy
Extension Class for playing inappropriately
with a Pritt Stick.
```

Next:

```
All Staff: Yeti found
```

Mentor came in and congratulated me.

'Progress!' she said.

'At last! Now for Good!' I declared. Then, tentatively, I asked, 'How do I become Good?'

'Why don't you go and watch VP?'

'I have done.'

'And?'

'Frankly, it was really boring.'

'For you maybe. How did the kids behave?'

'They were rapt. Immaculate.'

'There you are.'

'But it was just the same old slides! Arial, 18 point, blue for questions, green for answers. No alarms and no surprises. And here I am, with all my bells and whistles, breathing some fire into the fuckers, giving it the full Art

Tatum, and I get told, "Actually, can you just play 'Chop-sticks' over and over?"'

She nodded as if this was something she heard often.

'They may look the same, but look closely. Every lesson she has tweaked and tweaked. She has thought and re-thought every lesson to the point of mania. I have watched her spend three hours planning a Year 8 Set 3 lesson. She is always thinking about what they have just done in the last lesson, what they understand, and what they need to recap on. All those questions in the Starter are carefully tailored to consolidate the last lesson and to advance the learning at a pace the class is comfortable with.'

'Yeah, but where's the excitement?' I said. 'The passion? The imagination? Comprehensions every time? What is an adjective? Fuck that!'

'You're up there doing all your singing and dancing, and they're just getting overexcited. But they're not learn-ing anything. You need to stick to the formula. Starter, Main Task, Plenary. Bish, Bash, Bosh. It's like Pavlov's dog. When every lesson, in every discipline, is taught in exactly the same way, then student satisfaction and good behaviour will follow because they like the security of the routine, and it conditions their behaviour. Ding! Dog biscuits. Slobber. Never take a class over from her. Once you've had VP, you never go back.'

Lesson #99
Great Teaching Is about Routine,
Structure and Purpose.

Lesson #100
KISS - Keep It Simple, Stupid.

And so I put away my childish things and taught exactly the way VP taught.

I stormed up to class, a man on a mission. I imagined that the class I was walking into weren't kids, but a board-room of expectant investors.

Buy! Sell! Nail it! What's the Take-Out? Guys, I've got a plane to catch! What's the Bottom Line?

From then, I was preternaturally calm. A Zen Zeus. I stood still, front and centre; I scanned the room for the slightest infraction; if there was the tiniest movement, I disappeared the miscreant with a single gesture; I did not need to say a word. All the instructions were on the board. Up to this point, I had pooh-poohed Lesson Objectives, thinking them reductive nonsense. Now I was all over them. Suddenly, my lessons gained the same urgency, purpose and direction as my walk. I could feel it, and so could they. We could feel the collective thrum of learning happening. *We are going places, people! Get on the chara-banc of destiny!*

Every day, the same way.

Ding!
    Slobber.
    Questions.
    Answers.
    Clarity.

Structure.
Security.
Success.
Progress.
Confidence.
Calm.
Plenary.
Post-it.
Get it?
Got it.
Good.
GOOD.
Oh, Good.
At last.
Wag wag wag.

7

Salim

I think that Narcissus is really vain and when I say vain I mean really vain.

Hmm. I'm not sure I can give him any marks for that. I guess he made a point. He just needs some evidence. And a proper explanation. And to vary his vocabulary. Tick. One mark.

He was getting there, mind. He understood the formula. And he was filling the lines. I gave their books back and celebrated him as much as I could.

As they had been good – and so had I – I decided to let them go to the computer room to create a Facebook page for their favourite god or goddess, which for them was like the bestest thing ever. They leapt and skipped and whispered excitedly as we walked down the stairs, then scurried to their places.

You have to be ultra-vigilant in computer lessons, because one click and they open Pandora's Box. They sat for an hour, without looking up, placated and zombified. Five minutes before the end of the lesson, I told them to print off their work. I thought this would be an easy process. Couple of minutes, tops. It took forever – I had to tell them which printer to select ten times and there were the inevitable paper jams – so we drifted into break. Their work was vivid if underwhelming: a series of fluorescent slides with images of alabaster gods at jaunty angles; skulls and hearts dotted around; random facts about gods cut and pasted from Wikipedia; the Facebook logo splashed across the middle.

They rushed off into the playground, shouting, 'Bye, Sir!' and 'Thanks, Sir!' and 'Can't wait for the next computer lesson, Sir!' I watched them as they dissipated into the world: Mercedes ran straight to her friends who held the skipping rope, jumping straight in; Milosz joined his friends under the tree and ate chocolate; Kieran put on his big Puffa and joined the other Puffas in the corner of the playground, gently swaying from foot to foot as they surveyed the playground with incipient swagger. As I tried to arrange the papers into some semblance of order, I had a sense that someone was standing too close to me. Salim.

He wanted to stay behind and talk about his god, Nataraja. I had some detainees for break, so I ushered them to their desks, then sat down with Salim and looked at his work. He was nervous to begin with, but quickly became impassioned as he took me through it. There were photos of statues of Nataraja, the Hindu Lord of the Dance, dancing the Dance of Bliss within an arch of flames, a cobra uncoiled from his right arm. Salim had provided a couple of annotations – denoted with large yellow arrows, bigger than the god itself – with blue hyperlinks within them, explaining that Nataraja was 'the cosmic dancer who performs his divine dance to destroy a weary universe and make preparations for the god Brahma to start the process of creation!!!!!' He stuttered and widened his eyes as he tried to convey the astonishment of it all. The dance is 'the source of all movement within the universe' and 'the purpose of his dance is to release the souls of all men from the snare of illusion!!!!!!!'

I knew Salim was special. When teachers say that, they don't mean it in a derogatory sense. Quite the opposite.

I knew he was special the first time I saw him in the playground, standing apart from everyone, watching and counting the skipping, his toes pointing inwards. From that point on, I always talked to him when I was on duty. Not because I felt sorry for him, but because he always had an interesting take on the world. He regaled me with storylines from Bollywood films and showed me the dance moves.

For a while, I was his only friend, which became problematic. When I walked past my hard-earned quiet line outside the classroom, a voice would pipe up: 'Hello, Sir. I have been here for five minutes'; or 'Hello, Sir. I have written five lines for homework.' I told him to be quiet, and that if he spoke again, he would get a detention. Everyone knew he wouldn't.

At the beginning of term, his hand was always up. When he spoke, he leaned back his eyes lit up, and a robotic voice emerged. He had tried to befriend various members of the class, but now they ostracised him. One by one, his partners had peeled away. Now he sat on his own, and it was very difficult to find anyone to work with him.

All the signs were there: the social awkwardness; the obsession, particularly with numbers; the literal approach to texts. He couldn't handle it when the bus was late; when it rained; when I didn't reward them with Haribos, like I said I would. The boundaries, rules and regular ritual of the school were great comfort to him. He flourished in an environment in which everything was kept as regular as possible. But we could not keep all irregularities at bay. Sometimes the lasagne did not stay rigid and collapsed over his green beans; sometimes I said I would give the books back on Wednesday and gave them back on Thursday; sometimes I gave them 12 minutes to write rather than 15. These were all egregious irregularities that exposed me as a liar, and the world as unstable and unpredictable.

Lesson #107
Don't Speak Metaphorically
to Autistic Children.

We were told this during our training, but it is easy to forget. For instance, a teacher had told an autistic pupil that he was 'on fire', because he was working so hard; the kid leapt up, shouting, 'I'M ON FIRE! HELP! I'M ON FIRE!' I thought of this when I told the class that they could finish two pieces of work, and kill two birds with one stone. Salim looked at me with a pained expression, and said, 'I didn't kill any birds!'

I ensured I explained things as clearly and concretely as I could, with as few words as possible, repeating myself slowly, having the instructions clearly written on handouts and on the board. The handouts were simple and colourful: images of characters or concepts, with boxes underneath providing sentence starters or connectives. Teaching Salim forced me to unravel the whole process of instruction and start again. I could take nothing for granted. For every stage of a lesson, I had to make sure that I was absolutely clear, that I was going at a pace that he was comfortable with, and that he was secure in his understanding (for example, by saying 'thumbs up or thumbs down', or letting them show the green, yellow or orange pages in their Planners to show the level of their understanding without being exposed to the rest of the class).

Thus Salim made me a better teacher of the whole class. They all benefited from such careful, well-planned differentiation. I realised that I had been going too fast and assuming too much of everyone in the class. Now they were all with me for the whole lesson. Pace is one of the most difficult things to master.

Lesson #115
You Are Going Too Fast.

Almost all beginner teachers go too fast. It takes a great deal of skill to go at a pace which everyone in the class is comfortable with, which combines fast-paced attention-grabbing engagement with slow consolidation and repetition. True differentiation involves setting different levels of the same task, so that pupils can go at their own pace.

The question was whether Salim benefited by being in there with the others. On the one hand, you could say his socialisation was being improved (a moot point if every other child is teasing him and refusing to sit with him). On the other, he would surely benefit from targeted one-on-one, and we had an excellent autism unit with superb specialists and resources. I needed a permanent TA to help out. It was time for Paula.

'Y'a'right, Sir?'

She was always smiling. She laughed whenever she saw me, partly because she was a happy person, but I am sure that a part of her was laughing at me.

She had worked all over. All manner of schools. Nice ones, nasty ones. And here the longest. She knew all the Old Guard, and always had a knowing wink and a laugh with her old friends from 'the old school'. When it was real. When it was like family.

'Now, these young teachers, well. They're just like kids, ain't it? They look barely old enough to be my son! Don't get me wrong, I like them. They get results. But most of them just don't got time to sit and chat. To have a chin-wag. You know? That's what it is all about.'

The one thing she really knew was that whatever changed – the building, the Head, the money, whatever – none of it don't matter, because the one thing that stays constant is that 'kids is kids is kids'.

And she should know. Teachers should suffer from the curse of empathy. But, in reality, we only have time to flag up those we feel are in need of support, then hand them over. We don't have enough time to talk about the work, let alone what is really going on in their heads. She's the one who has to really empathise.

She was always following at least one student around. Some were in wheelchairs, some shuddered along on walking frames, some ran around pell-mell. You would see her helping them into the lift or escorting them to the toilet. Or sitting with them, explaining the same things over and over and over again.

I saw her at lunchtime, supporting a child on a walking frame. We were at the back of a huge queue, which had developed into a scrum, as every child in the school was attempting to get their lunch. She was barged and jostled by Year 9s as she slowly and deliberately stacked up a tray for the pupil.

'Ya want chicken pie? What about crumble?'

She looked at the chef and winked.

'Y'a'right?'

'Yes, Paula! Y'a'right? How you been?'

'Fine. Fine.'

'Sorry it took so long. Ya shoulda come right to the front! Ya should know that by now!'

She cackled and wagged her finger.

'Ya know me. Anyway. The last shall be first. And the first shall be last.'

The moment she stepped into my class, everything changed.

She came in at the beginning of the lesson, but she made a point of not being with Salim, so he didn't feel self-conscious. To begin with, she looked out of the window, uninterested, half listening. Once they had begun a task, she slowly circulated, peering over the kids' shoulders. Some TAs freak kids out when they do this. The worst are the really abrasive ones who start shrieking at the kids to get on with it, winding them up and creating a scene. Some put you off by staring at their phones, monged with boredom. Some even call out to correct things you've said. Mick used to come in and shout, 'What's that say? I can't read it. What's this lesson about, anyway? I haven't got a clue. Have you? Nah, me neither. Sir! What you on about?'

Paula barely spoke. She did not need to. Everything was met with a slow nod, a calm tap on the page. Come on. Let's get on.

She made a point of sitting next to every kid. They all had spaces next to them, after all.

Kieran got a bit shirty to begin with.

''Low it, leave me alone!'

She joked with him, pretended to take his pen. She knew when to turn on the humour. When he got the pen back he was keen to show her that he was not fooling around and really wanted to write.

Mercedes knew her from outside school. Another parent *in loco*. Soon she was desperate to show her how much she had done. Whenever Paula arrived, she proudly held up her page.

'Look how much ya done, Mercedes! Look at you!'

Mercedes beamed.

Milosz kept looking around – out of the window, at his shoes, anywhere but at his book. She sat next to him until he was becalmed. She tapped on the page. He looked at her. Then he started to write. She got up again when he had written a complete sentence and nodded to me.

When she reached Salim, she craned her neck casually to see over his shoulder. Whenever I did this, he became self-conscious and covered up his work. But with Paula, he confessed that he did not know what he was supposed to be doing. She quietly took him outside and they finished the task on the table outside the classroom with no fuss and no attention drawn.

By the time the lesson was over, he had finished three questions and was smiling.

'Thank you, Miss. Hasn't he done well?' I said.

'Thank you, Sir. See you next time.'

She walked down the hall and into another classroom.

8

Smile, It's Christmas

Year 7s clustered in the playground, protecting each other from the cold wind, like yaks on the tundra. Women in woolly hats and tights nursed hot cups of tea. Hubristic PE teachers in shorts and trainers did squat jumps, grunting and punching the air. The kids laughed. A chorus of 'Oh, my daze!'

A whistle blew. The clusters dispersed and then filed into lines with the startling efficiency and grace of a starling murmuration. Kids nestled their chins into the collars of their jackets, mouthed smoke rings into the air. Suddenly, their faces were illuminated by strobe flashes of light, then a steady glow, as classroom lights around the playground were turned on with an ambient hum.

VP stood at an end of one of the lines, surveying the troops before they went Over the Top. A whistle blew again. The hush of anticipation and fear.

One by one they were picked off. Moving out of line. Disorganisation. Wrong equipment. Insubordination.

'Morning, Dear,' whispered Tom.

Morning DEAR – Drop Everything and Read – was the new literacy boondoggle to get the Year 7s reading. They were not reading in their own time, so we were going to open their eyes to the Classics by forcing them to read at gunpoint before school every morning when they were freezing cold and half asleep. In order to qualify, I had to go and read *Winnie the Pooh* to VP, which was chilling and horrific, but I got the gig.

The PE teachers ended up being the best at the job, partly because kids love guys in shorts who shout and have bantz; they were also essentially on the same level as the Year 7s when it came to literacy. There were various Maths teachers too, although they seemed to be in it solely for the free croissants.

It soon became a highlight of my day. The kids slumped in, eyes still puffy, and plonked their bags on the desk. Donnie leaned on his bag; Mercedes stared out of the window; Salim took out his things in the same order he always did; Milosz rested his head in the crook of his elbow; Chika opened her book and started reading immediately.

This was the magic hour. The only time in the day when I had them at my mercy. They were in the liminal state between waking and sleeping – the best time to read and dream. And quietly, deliberately, selflessly, we read beautiful stories. From this point onwards, the day would offer nothing but distractions and enervations that would take us all further and further away from ourselves. But, for now, I could be gentle. I did not have to bark or shout or wind them up. We could simply be, here, in this room, with this book, in this blessed quiet respite from chaotic lives and oppressive expectations. A book that I had not broken down into gobbits, or set comprehensions and essays on, or provided a series of images or videos that created precisely the wrong effect. We did not have to rush through it. We did not even have to finish the first page. We could just discover it, together.

I always thought they hated it and resented me for getting them up early. I would have hated me. But one day, while reading *Alice in Wonderland*, I stopped suddenly, wondering if anyone was listening to me.

Kieran piped up, 'Don't stop!'

'Why?' I asked.

'It's relaxing.'

They all agreed.

'Yes, reading is relaxing. That's the main point of it.'

'Yeah. We should do more of it.'

Boom ting.

Kieran loved *Noughts and Crosses*; Donnie *The Hunger Games*; Chika devoured Harry Potter, much to her mother's chagrin (she didn't approve of his brand of magic); Mercedes liked *Junk*. She thought it was even better than 'the blubs' (I think she meant the blurb). She even took the book out and read it every night at home. She was my big breakthrough.

Mercedes used to stand in line outside the classroom, combing the front of her afro down over her eyes, making provocative observations on anything that wandered past her limited vision, growling and gurning and grizzling like a generator. She had to make a point of saying something – anything – just before she reached the threshold of the classroom. It became a game. I stood beside the classroom door, greeting them as they entered; she always piped up 'A'right, Sir!' or 'Sir, wa'gwan?', knowing I could not respond; knowing I was sworn to silence; knowing I had to keep shtum until everyone was behind their desks; knowing I was being watched more than she was.

But there was a lot of front, and it was as fragile as gossamer. Underneath was broiling rage and confusion. Sometimes I saw tears appear when reading. And then, quick as a flash, they were wiped away as she launched into a tirade against someone. Like everyone else in that class, she covered her vulnerability with braggadocio. I could not stop the class and demand that we all 'just talk about what is really bothering us'. That was for Circle Time. She was an attention-seeker *par excellence*, what we call a great 'tester of limits'. Her disruption and antagonism were pleas for friendship. But I had to maintain uniformity of expectations. She knew she could push me so far – a wry, knowing smile, an arched eyebrow – and then just as I was about to go nuclear, she reined it in.

I planned the opening of my lessons around harnessing her volatile, scattergun energy. The Starter had to be interesting, challenging, fun: a puzzle, a word game, a challenge. Quickly, she was buzzing: 'Ooh, ooh, I know this!'; 'Ooh, ooh, I got it! I got it!' Almost immediately both arms were stretching to the sky, contorting her face into bizarre expressions, imploring, 'Pick me! Pick me!' The trick was to galvanise the energy she had when she entered the room, but not so much that the whole class was disrupted. I had to celebrate her when she got the first challenge right, and then hope the positive energy would carry through the next task, whereupon she could lift the more sedate members of the room. But then I faced the danger of it all going tits up when she started getting arrogant and bossing people around or treating them like they were stupid. I was ready to start attempting some paired work, but I had to be very careful about who I let her be in a pair with. She couldn't go with Milosz or Saadia because she intimidated them; she couldn't go with Chika because Chika would do all the work, although Mercedes would take the credit; she couldn't go with Salim because he couldn't go with anyone; if I tried to put her with Donnie she would shake her arms dramatically and say, 'NO! NO! NO'; Kieran wanted to do paired work with Mercedes more than anything, but she led him on and didn't focus, so I had to keep them apart, which made Kieran rebel more. I ended up mixing it up, and letting her go with a different kid each lesson. Gradually, they learned to tolerate each other. Maybe even like each other, a little.

Now the SMs were off my back, I got to spread my wings ever so slightly and try some of the strategies I had learned from my training. We did 'thought tracking' (verbalising the character's thoughts), cloze exercises (cutting up poems or paragraphs and getting the kids to rearrange them in the correct order) and scaffolded creative writing, in which they were told to write their own myths, with the support of differentiated worksheets, sentence starters and sophisticated vocabulary. The secret was to come up with a variety of quick tasks, because they lost focus so fast. It was incredible how they just couldn't sit still, like there were ferrets loose in the class running up their legs. When they started to jiggle, I borrowed Tom's strategy, which was to get them to do very quick aerobics – hands up, to the side, down below, up above – in order to refocus. I had to do this exercise three times a lesson, at least.

During the individual work, they were learning to stay relatively quiet and focused. It was all about managing my expectations: rather than insisting they write for fifteen minutes to produce half a page, I realised that eight minutes and five lines was about their limit. And those eight minutes were blissful. Like reading, the quiet concentrated time became addictive.

Their success was also addictive. By writing an extra two lines in class or for homework, they rose by a level. That then spurred them on to write more the next time. And when they saw that they could rise by another level by correcting their work in the Plenary, they focused even more. Donnie stayed behind every lesson to redo his homework in break or after school. For others in the class it was more about the competition. It was all about the levels. Every lesson, when I gave the books back, they would say, 'What did I get?' and turn immediately to the mark. They didn't read what I had written. Just saw the mark, and whether it was better than everyone else.

Lesson #125
Sadly, Competition Is the Motivator.
Particularly for Boys.

I learned from the more experienced members of the Department some simple strategies for capitalising on their competitiveness and giving them pride in their work. For instance, you can cut out photos of the kids from the register and superimpose them onto super-heroes. Or you can scan examples of their work so they have to identify whose work was the best. Soon they were jostling for who could be put on the board, who would be the King or Queen of Homework, or Classwork, or Be-haviour, or whatever.

The competition even unlocked Kieran for a while. He did not want to learn, necessarily; he just wanted to cease failing. And then beat everyone else. I printed off his work, turned him into a superhero. His marks slowly crept up, his confidence grew. The other members of the class con-gratulated him and asked him for help. He glowed with this strange new sensation of pride, particularly when Mercedes paid him attention. Soon, every aspect of his attitude changed: he was punctual, Puffa-less, diligent. On it.

Role play was also extremely effective. Just as a child might not talk to you about his or her feelings, but can tell the puppet on your finger, so the recalcitrant pupil will not come to the board as themselves. But dress them as an explorer and get them to report back from their travels, and you can't get them to shut up. That's how it was with my Year 8s when doing *His Dark Materials*. One group was astrologers, another Arctic explorers, another scien-tists. They had to report back on what they thought 'dust' was. All of them, loud and quiet alike, armed with the requisite vocabulary and terminology, were transformed into experts.

We had a mortar board and gown hanging in the classroom closet. At some point in the lesson, usually during feedback, I let them pretend to be the professor or expert. The very act of putting on the mortar board or gown made them feel special and respected. They loved to come to the board and use different colour pens to lead feedback (although Mercedes liked to write other inappropriate things). Even if they didn't know the answer, the act of writing other people's answers was empowering and kept them focused. Getting them to teach each other was the Holy Grail.

Lesson #132
You Must Teach Them to Teach Themselves.

This is one of the great paradoxes of teaching. Once you have all your classes teaching each other, you are Outstanding. Literally. You are surplus to requirements. You have realised your own built-in obsolescence. Like Obi-Wan, you can martyr yourself, safe in the knowledge that the Force is being propagated.

We finished the Greek Myths with Perseus, a myth set a long time ago, when fortune-tellers told the truth.

Their task was to debate what the noblest kingdom in the world would look like. Donnie suddenly piped up, 'Like this!' And everyone went 'Yeah!'

The class debated what made our class great. Kieran said it was the uniform (which was odd, given that he spent most of his time disguising it with a Puffa); Salim said it was that they felt safe; Saadia said they loved learning; Donnie said, 'Because this is great! I love this class! It's like Limpix! Everyone achievin', everyone equal!'

I was close to tears.

That's how I feel, deep down. Like a realisation of the utopian visions of George Dennison in *The Lives of Children* or John Dewey in *Democracy and Education*: a projection of the society we want to realise. This room – all these rooms – are microcosms of how I want the world to be. A more equal, diverse, tolerant, respectful, generous, intimate and funnier society. One in which kids come from everywhere, and everywhere is as valuable as everywhere else; where the dominant culture is one of learning and respect for learning. Within – no, *throughout* – these sacred glass walls, we are equal. Will we ever be again?

I looked around for an SM, but of course they never come when you have moments like that.

I was buzzing as they left. Donnie hung around, awkwardly.

'You can go now,' I said. 'You're not in trouble. I didn't give you a detention. Did I?'

'No, Sir. I just . . . wanted to do some homework. Can I do some homework?'

'Of course.'

I noticed he had a bruise on his cheek. I asked him how he got it. He said he walked into a door.

I filled in a Cause for Concern form, a form you have to fill in when you are concerned for a child's welfare, which is seen only by the Head of Year.

There was levity in the staff room, both forced and un-forced. SMs and TAs occasionally poked their heads in wearing Santa hats or reindeer antlers. Mentor had draped tinsel all over the windows and put a little tree on top of the fridge. There were sweets everywhere. Haribos, Fruittellas, Maltesers, Mini Mars, Mini Snickers, Lindt. Bananaman couldn't believe his luck.

Teaching took a bath. We were all so done with teaching. It was just tests, tests, tests until Christmas.

I handed out the tests to the Set 1s, and they started writing like they had been charged with writing all of Shakespeare in an hour.

I clicked on my emails.

There was a Christmas Tombola for the PTA.

An envelope spun around, enlarging until it was the size of the screen, with fancy calligraphy writing embossed on it: 'You are cordially invited to the Christmas Party!'

I clicked on it. The envelope opened and a champagne bottle exploded and balloons flew around the screen.

DJs! And Dancing! And a Buffet! On a Boat!

Lots of email bantz followed from teachers who scorned it but for whom it was, in fact, the highlight of their social calendar.

We converged on the Library even earlier the Friday of the party. The PE department was leading the charge, looking slightly odd in clothes that weren't shorts, like Ben Sherman shirts, jeans and brown loafers.

HoD bought the shots. Given that I was in my training year (and therefore still 'on probation'); given that I was going to be with my immediate superiors, all of whom had passed some form of negative judgement on me over the term; and given that we would be in a small, enclosed space that we could not escape from for four hours . . . it made total and utter sense for me to get really shitfaced.

Onboard the boat, I was overcome by the tinsel, laughter, throbbing hip hop, sausages on sticks and ironic sweaters.

Double take.

Off-duty SM.

Laughing, drinking, sweating, flirting.

Even more sinister.

Walls coming in.

Everything wobbly.

Wooah.

I tried to focus on Tom, who looked in equally bad shape.

The TAs were DJing and dancing everyone off the floor. Little Miss Outstanding ran up to me and shouted, 'I'M DANCING WITH THE TAS. I'M DANCING WITH THE TAS!'

Tom made the universal gesture of smoking, so we went on deck to get some air. I realised I was standing right next to VP ranting about the meeting she had had that day when they selected the next cohort of Year 7s.

'And I swear to God at one point I actually said, "I'll swap you one in a wheelchair with one with learning difficulties,"' she said.

Tom and I looked at each other, then quickly staggered back into the throng.

Need a drink.

Oh my God.

Oh. My. God.

SM dancing.

Quick.

Oh my God.

I pushed through the crush to the bar.

Oh shit.

VP.

Try to appear normal.

Ask her a question.

'Got anything planned for Christmas?'

(Nice, bland opening gambit.)

'Rearranging my filing cabinet.'

What am I supposed to do with that?

'Always the highlight.'

'Can I get you a drink?'

'I'm fine. Thanks.'

I am just grinning at her like a maniac.

'Hey. You know you said, "Don't Smile Until Christmas"? Well, look! It's Christmas! And I can't stop!'

You didn't just say that.

You. Didn't. Just. Say. That.

'Quite right. You have every right to. It's all up from here.'

'WIN WIN EVERY TIME!'

I hugged her. I may have kissed her.

'Merry Christmas!'

'Merry. Christmas.'

I was released. The hardest term was over. It felt like it had been an entire year. Maybe three. I was ready to retire.

The holidays came and went. I slept for the first week, promising myself every day that I would mark all the books I had brought home in giant tote bags, but they just sat in the corner of my room, staring at me with quiet resentment. After a few nights' recuperation, I returned to a semblance of myself and realised how shot my body was. My back was crippled from all that book carrying, my shoulders were crook from yanking my arms behind my back, my feet were blistered from the rub of the brogues, and my thighs were raw from all that purposeful walking.

I spent most of Christmas lunch trying to answer the boilerplate questions from my extended family ('Must be so rewarding?', 'Do they come from all over?'), but I had forgotten the whole term already.

Dad wasn't well. He spent Christmas lunch on the sofa. After lunch, I sat beside him and told him about my school, and about what I was teaching. I could tell he was delighted I had followed in the family tradition, that he had successfully 'passed it on'. He knew that teaching provided nourishment for my starving soul, and I saw tears in his rheumy eyes as I talked about it. He remembered what it was like, the ineffable joy.

His father had been an English teacher, who was able to communicate with his children only through literature. It was the same with me and Dad. I remember walking across the fields at sunset as he recited 'Ye elves of hills, standing lakes and groves' from *The Tempest*. Meant nothing to me at the time. Now I can't read it enough.

He stared at me silently with a wincing smile. At one point, I said, 'Look, Dad, I hope you are proud of me. I have tried to do what you wanted. To be the man you wanted . . .'

He stared at me. I became all choked up and couldn't speak any more.

We stared into the fire, serene.

9

Parents' Evening

The gym reverberated with the hubbub of a bustling street market. Before me was a line of expectant customers. I felt like I should have a table of wares – yams, plantains, cumin, fine silks, broken-spined Penguin classics, Wedgwood teapots. I had a spreadsheet. Fathers, mothers, brothers, sisters and carers stood before me, their charges standing limply beside them.

The meetings followed the same pattern, to begin with. I sang the kid's praises, citing specific work; discussed homework, how and where it was done; encouraged involvement in music and theatre; and finally, a little bit of pastoral ('Is there anything we need to know?'). My final question was always the same: 'I know what you are reading at school, but what do you have by your bedside?'

I had to see both classes in one evening, so was going to have to be swift and efficient. First up were the Set 1s.

'Hello. I'm Mrs Foley. Orlando's mum.' A woman with frizzy hair in a green kaftan sat down. 'Thank you so much for teaching him this term. He really, really enjoys English. Don't you, Orlando? (He's not going to say anything. Not while Mum's here.)'

She whispered dramatically behind her hand: '*Between you and me. I think he needs a little pick-me-up. Been a bit down in the dumps.*'

I tried to meet Orlando's downcast gaze.

'Orlando. You've been top of the class all term.'

'No, I haven't.'

'You have! You are one of the best in there.'

He harrumphed.

'*I think he thinks*', Mrs Foley continued, '*that Sam – is it Sam? – I think he thinks that Sam gets better levels.*'

'That's because he does,' grunted Orlando.

'I'm sorry to hear that, Mrs Foley, really I am.'

'He still has not recovered from the 6a you gave him for Icarus.'

Orlando shook his head and muttered, 'Should have used more varied language.'

And there it was. A tiny little phrase, one that I threw out ten times a day, usually as a sop to the arbitrary target system, and it had rankled and destroyed this poor boy from within.

'But that is the best level you can get!' I implored.

'I thought you gave Sam a level 7?' replied Mrs Foley.

'Yes, but that was a one-off. Something so extraordinary –'

'It's been very difficult, Mr Teacher, I have to tell you. He has hardly done anything since. Not practised piano or violin. He's a perfectionist, you see. Runs in the family, I'm afraid. You know his sister, in Year 12? The composer? My husband thinks – I'm sorry he can't be here tonight – he's delivering a lecture – he's a professor –'

'Yes, Orlando mentioned.'

A large queue was now stretching from my desk, blocking some of the other teachers' desks.

'Did he? Yes, I'm sure he did . . . Look, I don't want you to think I'm a Tiger Mother or something ghastly like that. I do just genuinely want him to be happy. But we're at our wits' end and I just wondered what you suggest?'

An SM hovered and then beat on.

'I'm sorry, Mrs Foley,' I said. 'I should never have given Orlando such high marks to begin with, because the only way is down. Truth is, I can't imagine there are many eleven-year-olds in the country currently producing such brilliant work. So please just chill out and try to enjoy reading and writing. The worst thing you can do is burn yourself out. And if you need to miss the odd essay, that's OK with me. I just want you to be happy.'

'Did you hear that, Orlando? Did you hear what Sir said?'

Orlando nodded.

I stood up and shook her hand.

'Thank you for everything you have done.'

'I haven't done anything,' I said, ushering them towards the next desk.

Femi sat down. He had a lovely, bright, cheerful face, and dressed immaculately. You are told not to have favourites, but it is very difficult not to. We all said he was like the son we would like to have.

Femi was from that rare breed who are hard-working, sweet, chatty, lively, moral and interested. He never missed a day's school, and was given a prize for that very feat. His book was immaculate. He would wait after each lesson and ask what he could have done better in his homework.

I had heard he had escaped great hardship, and had not been in the UK long. It was difficult to know what had happened. Sometimes he wrote stories of war and strife; one time he drew pictures of men with guns in military uniforms standing outside huts. Femi could not speak English when they arrived, and now here he was in Set 1.

His parents sat either side of him, like bookends. I told them that I couldn't believe how much he had come on, how proud they must be, how he was a credit to them. An example to us all. They nodded and beamed and said, 'Thank you, oh thank you, oh thank you.' I made him promise to try to speak a bit more in class. He promised he would through nervous smiles. I bade them farewell, with a profound sense of privilege; they were people for whom education was the most important thing in life.

Rachel lived round the corner from the school, so I had met Rachel's mum on the street.

'How's she getting on?' I asked, rhetorically.

'Not so good. I mean, she loves English. Yeah. She really likes it. Always has.'

'Good. She's very good at it.'

'Is she?'

'Yes! Absolutely.'

'There. You hear what Sir's saying? You're good!'

Rachel looked at her shoes.

'She doesn't feel like she's any good. She says that everyone else in the class knows everything. That they all read everything and that. And that they think she's stupid.'

'Mum!'

'It's true! That's what you said to me!'

I placated her. 'Nothing could be further from the truth. She has made fantastic progress this term.'

'That's brilliant, Rachel! You hear what Sir's saying?'

She fiddled with her shoe buckle.

'We just need to get her speaking a bit more in class. Don't we, Rachel?' I said, switching my focus from Mum to Rachel and back again. 'At the beginning of the year, she talked all the time in class. Always had her hand up. But recently . . . not a peep.'

'Same at home,' said her mum. 'She just comes home and then disappears upstairs. Sits on the computer all night. Dunno what she does up there.'

Rachel gradually came round. But I felt terrible that she felt so insecure and intimidated. We agreed that she should come see me after school to go through anything she didn't understand. Or when I saw her on my walk home.

After a short water break, it was time for the Set 4s.

Milosz sat down with his mum. He stared at me, already red-faced, with a look that said *Don't Say What You Are About To Say*.

Right. Time to give you a piece of my mind.

'Now, Mrs Brodowski. Milosz has not made a very good start, I am afraid. Not at all.'

Milosz started translating. She nodded.

'There was the incident, as you are aware, with the Pritt Stick.'

He translated. She nodded and smiled.

'You are aware he was caught committing the sin of Onan with a Pritt Stick in the back of Oracy Extension?'

He translated. She nodded and smiled.

'He really needs to focus more. To get on with what I set him to do. He really needs to pull his finger out.'

Mrs Brodowski was nodding and smiling.

What the hell is he saying to her?

'Milosz: are you translating what I am saying correctly?'

'Yes, Sir.'

'Are you sure? It seems to me that you must be saying very different things to the things that I am saying. If I was hearing what I was saying, I wouldn't be smiling and laughing. I would be frowning and getting cross.'

I began addressing her directly, trying to make my negative body language as clear as possible.

'Mrs Brodowski, I must impress upon you the need for Milosz to improve his attitude.'

I held up the spreadsheet and waved it beneath her nose.

'Look! Here! It's all red! It should be green but it is all red!'

She nodded and smiled.

'He is bright enough to go up a set. But he won't, not at this rate. He might go down.'

She nodded and smiled.

'Milosz, do you want to improve?'

'No,' he said, nodding and smiling.

I looked at his mother, who was smiling.

'OK. Nice to meet you.'

Salim sat down with his dad, and gathered himself, his knees touching each other, his palms neatly placed on each thigh. His father looked at me wearily, and told me how concerned he was. I told his dad that things were under control. That we would speak often. That he was in the best possible hands.

When Donnie's dad arrived, he looked me up and down suspiciously. I told him that Donnie had been staying at school to do his homework.

'Well, stands to reason, dunnit?' he said. 'You keep makin' 'im do all this work on computer. He ain't got no computer at home, 'as he? So now 'e's gotta stay at school to do it.'

I told him that he could do the work in his book if he wanted, but that he was choosing to stay at school. I said how proud I was with the improvement he had made.

'Yeah, well. I don't see it myself. What was that work he done the ovver day? Whatever. Somming. Anyway, I couldn't read your writing. And if I can't read it, then he certainly can't. Now I'm not bein' funny, but what chance 'as he got of improvin' if he can't read what you're writin'?'

I apologised and told him I would try to write clearly, but that he needed to be assured that his son was the most improved student in the class, and that he would go up a set next year.

'Yeah, well. I told ya he shouldn't be in that set wiv all those idiots. Should listen to me next time.'

Chika's mother wasn't happy with what Chika was reading. She said the Greek Myths were full of 'bad witches'. I said that we were going to do *Macbeth* and *His Dark Materials* in the subsequent years, and that witches and superstition featured in much of English Literature. She said she didn't want me to teach those books. I told her they were just stories. She told me to tell better stories. 'Like what?' I asked. 'Like the ones from the Bible,' she said.

Mercedes was happy to see me, and said, 'You gonna be nice about me, Sir, innit?' I said I was. She started combing her fringe. I told her carer that – while we had not got off to the best of starts – she was the most rewarding student I had taught that year. She was now focused and determined and producing excellent work. She had improved by such a degree that she was going to go up a set next year. She beamed, grizzled, and said, 'Fanks, yeah.' I asked what she had enjoyed the most from the year. 'Singing,' she said. (She was now officially labelled a 'Gifted and Talented' student.) Her carer agreed that singing in the Gospel Choir had made all the difference to her. I told her she had to carry on. And to keep reading!

I told Saadia's parents she needed to speak more in class. They didn't say anything.

Neither of Kieran's parents showed up.

I looked around. The hall was finally emptying. A few SMs were talking to parents. I watched Mercedes as she

walked through the double doors of the gym, and choked
back a rush of emotion. Totes emosh.

Lesson #148
Emotion Creeps Up on You.
You Have to Keep It in Check.

10

Fanks, Yeah

The kids were immaculate from Parents' Evening onwards. For two weeks, at least. Whenever they misbehaved, I said, 'Remember what we said at Parents' Evening?' and they got down to work. But after two weeks, no one could remember what was said at Parents' Evening. This is why it is best practice to call home every week, especially if you have something good to say, no matter how small – whether it is an idea they came up with in class or an act of kindness. Developing communication with parents is a vitally constructive element of education. I had kids in all my classes battling for who could do the best work or be the kindest or the most punctual; once they were, they would say, 'Can you call my mum?' Sometimes this became ridiculous, like when a kid would open a door for me, and then say, 'Can you call my mum?' It made me slightly concerned about how this reward of mum-calling would translate into the real world; in any other sphere of life, that would be a very odd interaction. Imagine leaving your job in a bank, and your fellow clerk opens the door for you. You thank him, and he says, 'Can you call my mum?'

Spring sprung; the days lengthened; it was no longer dark at the beginning or end of the day. A mood swept across Key Stage 3, which, while not exactly relaxed, was no longer batshit stressed. The stress had been pushed upwards, like a bolus of pus, towards Key Stages 4 and 5. The SMs were now all over GCSE and A Level classes like bacilli around vulnerable blood cells.

I had fun with my classes at last. I was on a level with them where they could take the piss out of me, and ask me questions about my life. Break through the carapace. Reveal the secrets. They like nothing more than bantz about Sir's or Miss's personal life. You don't have to say much. Just bat back their manic questioning occasionally with a dry rejoinder.

'Has you got a wife?'

'No. Look at his finger!'

'Doesn't mean he don't have a wife!'

'Yes, it does! You gotta have a ring to get married!'

''E's got a girlfriend! 'E said so! Innit, Sir, you gotta girlfriend?'

'OOOOOHHHHH! Sir's got a girlfriend! Sir's got a girlfriend!'

'You got a picture? Lemme see!'

'Is she as fit as Persephone?'

'Or Beyoncé?'

'Yeah! Sir's got swagger!'

'Is it Miss?'

'LOW IT!'

'Yeah, blatantly it's Miss.'

'Do you go pub and get WAVY wiv her?'

'Does she buy your ties?'

'Where do you live?'

'Where?'

'How dja get there? In a plane?'

'Has they got chicken and chips dere?'

'Don't you ever go chicken and chip shop for kissy-kissy time?'

'Naah, he's too busy gettin' WAVY wiv Miss! Sir, you're bad, you know. I'm gonna tell Miss dat you got a wife at home while you're leading her on.'

'Sir! You're bad you know. I was talkin' to Miss. Innit, Sir, you're mentally unstable?'

If you can deal with that at rapid fire, you will become quite the Bantosaurus.

At the end of a lesson in which we just shot the breeze, Kieran said, 'Why can't we always do this?'

I told him I had no idea. But then I thought about it, and realised that if every lesson was like this, then not every lesson would be like this.

The kids were much more settled with each other. Mercedes changed her fringe. Chika finished all the Harry Potters, despite her mother. Milosz began to speak more in class. Saadia still wouldn't say boo to a goose. Salim no longer needed to go outside the classroom to do his classwork; Paula even cajoled him into working with other kids, who were beginning to appreciate him as his confidence grew. Donnie worked and worked and worked, staying behind every day to do homework, even if he didn't have any. I was proud of them. They had made great progress, even if I had made up their levels so they were in line with the ridiculous predictions of what they should be getting.

'You are only as happy as your most unhappy child' is an old saw of parenting. The same is true of teaching. It

doesn't matter if the majority of your pupils have suc-
ceeded, and become happy, sociable, successful kids. You
will only remember the failure.

Kieran's purple patch didn't last too long. One Monday
he came in surly and slumped down at the back of the
class, without taking his Puffa off, hugging his rucksack
to his chest. I could tell the wheels had come off the bus
over the weekend. Mondays are like that.

He refused to work all week, spent every day in detention, falling further and further behind in his work.
He didn't seem to care; he no longer saw the point in
improving, or in being in school at all. Paula took him
out of lessons, but he was rude and recalcitrant when
he was with her. All of his teachers logged complaints
on the school's network, most of which were filed under
'Attitude'.

'Gave me a dirty look as he came in. When I told him to
come in again, he sucked his teeth. Gave him a detention.'

'Refused to work. Gave detention.'

'Distracting other students. Gave detention. Talked
back. Gave Late Det.'

'Came in late, refused to take off Puffa. Talked back.
Sent to VP's office. Tried to call home. No response. Late
Det. Refused to work. Week of Late Dets.'

We prided ourselves on not letting any kid fall through
the net and never giving up. But when there is no support at home it is very difficult. His attitude deteriorated
to such a degree that it was difficult to see him lasting. He
was a ticking time bomb.

We had been working on *Holes* by Louis Sachar. This is the story of Stanley Yelnats IV, an overweight teenage boy from a poor family who is wrongly accused of stealing a pair of shoes. He is sent to Camp Green Lake, a juvenile prison in the middle of the Texan desert, where he must dig holes that are exactly five feet deep by five feet wide because it 'builds character'. The family suffer from a 'hex', an inheritance from Stanley's 'no-good-dirty-rotten-pig-stealing-great-great-grandfather', who was made to carry a pig up a hill in Latvia to win the heart of his beloved. He escapes to America, bringing the curse with him.

We drew maps of Camp Green Lake. I asked what they thought the digging was a metaphor for.

Silence.

Please tell me they know what a metaphor is.

It's not like I don't tell them every lesson.

It's not like I have taught them *anything else*.

Chika said, 'It is a simile without "as" or "like".'

Zackly.

Milosz said, 'It's a metaphor for school.' I asked him to go on. He said, 'Well, because you are made to do this thing over and over again, but you don't know why.'

Boom ting.

Is that what school is?

Yeah!

Should it be?

No!

I asked what they really thought of school.

Kieran sucked his teeth.

'Rubbish,' he said, as he sunk deeper into his Puffa.

Mercedes said, 'Nah, nah, it's all right, you know.'

'Shut up. Wha' you sayin? Suck-up.'

'Come den.'

'Why do you hate this, Kieran?' I asked. 'You used to love books.'

'Some loser pushin' a pig up a hill. Like dat guy who pushes a rock up a mountain. Who cares?'

I asked him if it reminded him of school. He shrugged and looked out of the window.

To illustrate how oracular stories are passed on, I asked them to play Chinese whispers. A story was whispered around the room, passed from partner to partner, and then Chika told the final story to the class. It was completely different from the original story. Helpless giggles ensued. For the rest of the lesson, I made them write stories about travelling to another country. They wrote them up in their books for homework.

The next lesson I decided to broach race and immigration in an attempt to integrate some 'British Values'. It was something I had been avoiding – my classroom was the 'noblest kingdom' in the world, after all, an enlightened, label-less, wall-less palace of light – but recently, I had noticed they were becoming more aware of what made them different.

I put up a slide with images of refugees and immigrants on the board and asked them to brainstorm. After a couple of minutes, I asked who wanted to come to the board. Mercedes's hand shot up. I was pleased to pick her; this had become her thing.

Mercedes bowled up to the front of the class, took the red pen and wrote 'FRESHY' in massive letters across the board. I asked her to explain what she meant.

'Dey're all freshies.'

'Who are?'

'All the Eastern Europeans and Africans.'

Er . . . quick. Pull out. Abandon ship. Next slide. Semi-colons. Anything.

Chika looked hurt. Milosz bridled. He was usually scared of Mercedes, and averted his gaze from hers, but this time he stared her down. She sucked her teeth at him. He muttered something under his breath in Polish. Mercedes lurched across at him and screamed in his face, gesticulating like a windmill. Donnie said, at the end of the day, they were all freshies, and he was the only proper English kid there. Everyone turned on Donnie. Kieran joined in – not because he was particularly exercised by the issue, more because it was a chance to be disruptive – and soon the whole room was reverberating with caterwauling and stomping. I had never heard them so incensed. Even Saadia was getting involved, and I hadn't heard her speak all year. Mercedes pushed Milosz out of his chair. She was swiftly disappeared. Chika screamed as loud as she could at Donnie. Donnie threw a book at Chika. There was a brief lull in the shouting as I heard Kieran shout at Saadia that he was going to 'wipe his arse on her headscarf'. He was disappeared all the way to VP's office.

I gave the rest of the class a stern talking-to. I told them they were all in detention and that I would be speaking to their parents and that I was very, very disappointed.

That was bad.
That was really, really bad.

Lesson #144
Just When You Think You're in the Clear, They Bite You in the Arse.

In detention, they had to write about a worse punishment than digging holes. While they were doing that, I called home.

'Hello. Is that Milosz's mum?'

'Yes?'

'Hi. This is Milosz's English teacher?'

'Yes.'

'Hi. I just wanted to talk about what happened in English today.'

'Yes.'

'He won't be home for a while, because he is staying here at school with me.'

'Yes.'

'It is a shame, because I have noticed a real improvement in Milosz's behaviour and attitude recently. Really. He is contributing much more in class. In fact, too much. Today, things got out of hand and he said some things which are frankly unacceptable. I didn't understand them all. But he ended up shouting at other students. There was a fight. He needs to learn to control himself.'

'Yes.'

'OK, well, I am just letting you know. That he is here.'

'Yes.'

'So you are happy for him to come home alone?'

'Yes.'

'OK, good to talk to you, Mrs Brodowski.'

'Hello. Is that Chika's mum?'

'Yes?'

'This is her English teacher.'

'Wha' 'appen?'

'Nothing. No, nothing. Well, something. There was a little problem in English today. We were talking about immigration and things got out of hand. Chika wasn't the main perpetrator, but she did start shouting –'

'I do not like this book.'

'No?'

'No. What are these curses? What are you teaching them?'

'They're just made up.'

'Why are you teaching things that are made up?'

'Er . . . that's my job.'

'Hello. Is that Donnie's dad?'

'Yeah. 'Oo's 'is?'

'This is Donnie's English teacher.'

'Wasseedone?'

'Well, we had a bit of a scene in English today. We were talking about immigration and Donnie became quite . . .

animated. He shouted and threw a book at a student. I have him here in detention.'

'Oh, right. 'Ave you now? Don't sound like 'is fault. Wasn't Donnie's fault. Sounds like all them other idiots. You need to get tough on 'em.'

'Donnie needs to control himself. Not get involved –'

'What, so 'e's not supposed to say nuffing if he is pro-voked? You're the teacher. You're supposed to be teachin' 'im 'ow to behave. Why you stirring them up like that?'

He's got a point.

'Hello. Is that Saadia's mum? I'm sorry. I'm so sorry. I am so, so, so sorry . . .'

Mercedes needed the next level up on the disciplinary ladder: Late Detention, followed by a raking over the coals with HoD and VP.

HoD, VP and I gathered in VP's office for the police procedural preamble: Mercedes waited in the purgatorial anteroom outside, while VP established the facts on the ground. I nervously explained what had happened, feel-ing increasingly guilty and inept. It's all the teacher's fault, after all. I should have prepared a lesson that headed off the race riot at the pass.

Mercedes was readmitted. We stared at her for some time, a triumvirate of doom. She glanced nervously from HoD to VP to me and back again, grinning slightly less with each glance.

VP began her Pintersque Inquisition, speaking even more deliberately and gravely than usual, leaving cavernous pauses to give Mercedes the opportunity to respond, playing Jedi mind-tricks, gently guiding her towards her ultimate admission of guilt.

'Why. Are. You. Here. Mercedes?'

She grizzled and stared at the floor.

'I am going to tell you what I know and then I want you to tell me what you know. Is that understood? OK. Mercedes. What happened in English this afternoon?'

She grizzled.

'You were supposed to be brainstorming. Is that correct?'

She nodded begrudgingly.

'Everyone in the class was working hard. *Working. Hard*. Because they want to succeed. Because they appreciate Sir's Outstanding teaching –'

I looked quizzically at HoD, who gave me a nod of benediction. This seemed an odd circumstance in which to be given some of the only praise I had yet received. It might only have been a mind-fuck to gull an eleven-year-old into making an admission of guilt, but I was going to take whatever I could get. Turns out, SMs always had your back in a Parental Meeting. They would go over the lesson in which there had been a behavioural incident and show the kid and the parent how the teacher had done exactly the right thing, even if you hadn't. It was tricky to get used to the paradoxical treatment you received from the SMs: in the context of parents, you were always right and the kid was lucky to have you as a teacher; in the context of other teachers, you were usually failing.

'And you decided . . . *You*. Decided . . . No one else . . . You. Decided. That this was the moment to come to the board. Yes? . . . And then once at the board you wrote a word . . . A word that you know is inappropriate and offensive. Is this correct?'

She grizzled.

'You knew. You. Knew. That you should not say this word, let alone write it on the board . . . You. *Knew*. This would cause the greatest disruption possible . . . A word which was very insulting. Why did you do it?'

Mercedes shuffled from foot to foot. She twisted her fringe, looking at each of us in turn, then grizzled something inaudible.

'I am sorry, Mercedes. I did not catch that.'

'Ssmsmfreshlikeastrawberry.'

'Please. Speak. Louder.'

'I meant they were fresh like a strawberry.'

Mercedes looked at me. At VP. At HoD.

I looked at HoD. At Mercedes. We all looked at VP. The Most Unflappable Woman in Christendom was not going to break.

'Fresh. Like. A. Strawberry?'

Mercedes grizzled and nodded.

'That is not an insult I am aware of. Sir? Is that an insult you are aware of?'

HoD shook his head.

'Sir? Is. That. An. Insult. You. Are. Aware. Of?'

I shook my head.

'No. That would be a nice thing to say to someone.' VP turned to me, her Jedi stare unwavering. 'If I said to you, Sir, that you are fresh like a strawberry . . . what would you say?'

Erm . . . I would be very freaked out indeed.

'I would say, "Thank you. That's very kind," I spluttered.

'You would, wouldn't you? You would be flattered. You might buy me flowers.'

I might. After I took you paintballing.

VP turned back to Mercedes.

'But that is not what you meant. Is it?'

'Yeah, it is,' she grizzled.

'Yes, it is, Miss.'

'Yes, it is, Miss.'

'No, it isn't, Miss, because you see, Mercedes, what you meant by that insulting curse word was that some of the other members of your class were fresh off the boat.'

'No.'

'Yes.'

VP tilted her head as her Jedi stare intensified.

'Yes,' said Mercedes.

'And I will not have such lack of respect in this school.'

Mercedes was given a week of Late Detentions.

Kieran's offence was deemed so grave that we needed a Parental Meeting followed by a suspension. We finally tracked Dad down and explained the severity of the situation. He reluctantly agreed to come in.

Kieran waited outside VP's office as VP explained to Dad that we had tried to do our best for Kieran, that he had had many chances, but things were getting out of hand. Dad didn't give a shit. Just looked at us like we were the problem. VP gestured for Kieran to enter. He slouched in, sat down and stared at the table. VP read him the riot act.

Bad attitude, slippery slope, nearly Year 8 now, the choices we make now affect the rest of our life. Crush. Suffer. Burn.

Kieran didn't move. A long silence. Suddenly, Kieran leapt up and screamed, 'I DON'T NEED DIS SHIT!' in VP's face.

She stared implacably. 'Calm. Down. Kieran. Just. Sit. Down.'

Even Dad told him to calm down. But Kieran wasn't having any of it. He spat on the floor, punched the glass wall of the office, and stormed out. No one moved as a giant cobweb spread slowly across the shattering glass wall.

I saw Kieran's whole life play out in that moment. Excluded from school after school, crime, prison, the whole sorry shitshow. This was the most profound feeling of failure yet. We had tried to change the narrative, to deviate the river. But sometimes the torrent is just too strong.

Thus Kieran was excluded from the noblest kingdom in the world.

In the summer, we studied *The Pearl* by John Steinbeck. Like the Greek Myths, *The Pearl* is the perfect book for Year 7s of any ability. It is short, clear and full of deep wisdom about class and morality.

Kino is a pearl fisherman, like his father and grandfather before him. When his son is stung by a scorpion, he must find money to pay for the doctor, who will not see them as they are too poor. He finds 'the pearl of the world' at the bottom of the sea, a pearl as 'perfect as the moon'.

But their relative wealth and security bring danger, envy, corruption and death.

We imagined the perfect world in which Kino's family lived; we discussed the destruction of rural fishing villages in Mexico as a result of global warming and tourism; we created the songs they sing in the town – the songs to the fishes, the sea, the light, the dark, the sun, the moon, the Song of the Family. Mercedes won with her 'Song of Fam'. We talked about the baby getting sick – most of them had baby brothers and sisters so could understand how upsetting this would be. We wrote an essay on the despised doctor. We talked about corruption and greed and how money ruins the world and how crazy it was to make people pay for healthcare in crazy places like America. We wrote stories about finding the most valuable thing in the world. Their writing still had the imaginative openness they had at the beginning of the year, but now it had more control. They had learned to craft a story.

Like the town in *The Pearl*, a class is like an animal. It has a nervous system, head, shoulders, feet, 'a whole emotion'.

The Set 1s were now bullying Rachel – about her dyed hair, the fact she didn't know where Mexico was, her song. I moved her to the front to sit with Femi, who was sweet and generous to her, but I could sense the class making fun of her behind her back. I kept meaning to report it officially, but I never took it to the next level. I had no idea how bad it was. What we see in class is the tip of the iceberg, to quote the opening slide of my metaphor lesson. Once Rachel got home, she opened up Facebook to be faced by abuse.

One day, I walked past Rachel's house. She was with a bunch of naughty boys I recognised from Year 9. She greeted me warmly and said, 'That's my English teacher.' It felt good to be stopped on the street like this, like being some kind of local dignitary – a vicar or doctor or something. The boys laughed and asked me what she was like at English. I told them she was very good at English, and the boys all laughed at her.

And that was it. She stopped working, stopped caring. English was no longer her thing. The animal had turned on her, forced her to become someone else.

I was never told why she left – whether she was excluded or whether she left voluntarily – but I knew I would miss her and I felt like I had failed her. I never quite looked at those Set 1s the same way again. They had lowered her confidence by quietly, insidiously, bullying her, but because I was so caught up in the more explicit bad behaviour of the Set 4s, I had let it slide.

Lesson #160
Never Let Anything Slide.

As the end of term approached, cards from kids were pinned to the notice board in the Department, providing a new strain of the ubiquitous competitive virus.

Mirror, mirror, on the wall, who is the greatest teacher of them all?

Mentor and Tom had a few cards, but they only put up the funny, poignant or well-written ones. Little Miss Outstanding had already amassed at least ten cards above her desk, which said things like 'Dearest Miss. Thank you for everything you have done for me. You are so kind and funny and clever. You really are the best teacher ever!!! Please, please, please teach me next year!!! Your favourite student.'

There were no cards above my desk.

The last week of term was spent filling in end-of-year self-evaluations and raiding the store cupboards for dystopian novels I could teach Year 12 the following year. I couldn't find enough of the *1984*s or *Fahrenheit 451*s for my class because Little Miss Outstanding had gone in weeks before the end of term – long before she even knew she would be teaching Year 12 – and pilfered most of them. I knew where they were, mind. She was already appropriating Room 10 as her own room for next year – she was in there every break time, putting up her posters of Laura Marling and perching her fluffy wombat on the computer. I found the books in the cabinet at the back and then hid them on top of the cabinet in Room 11, way out of her reach.

I was going through all my final paperwork with Mentor; she was just about to officially rubberstamp me as a Qualified Teacher, when HoD barged in.

'Ah, newbie,' he said, a smirk spreading across his face.

'You can't call me that, any more.'

'All right, ring piece. Has Miss told you about your classes next year?'

'Not really. Other than I've got Year 12s. Dystopia.'

'Yeah, right. That's fine. Easy. How about a real challenge?'

At last. The Holy Grail. He's going to give me Year 13. *The Waste Land*.

'Next year we are setting up . . . I can't even say the words . . .'

'What?'

'Next year we are setting up . . . The MEEDJA DE-PARTMENT.'

'Oh, no.'

'Yes.'

'Oh God, no.'

'Come on . . .'

'Please, no . . .'

'It's the chance to set something up, big kudos, we are talking major responsibility . . .'

'Anything but that . . .'

'Come to Daddy . . .'

'Literally: Go. Fuck. Yourself.'

'Congratulations on becoming a teacher of Meedja Studies.'

I slumped into the chair and held my head in my hands.

'And who, pray, is my Head of Department?'

'You and Tom. The Dream Team.'

I couldn't believe it. All these years, I had been preparing myself to be a man of letters, a carrier of the culture, a lightning rod of erudition. MEEDJA? The very thing that I despised more than anything else. The very thing that was corroding their minds and souls.

'When did this happen?'

'Just the other day. Old Head was never going to sanction it. In fact, I remember telling him we needed a Meedja

Department, and he said, "Over my dead body." Well, he's gone now. The new guy is only too happy to get rid of all that fusty crap like Classics. The Latin teacher was getting pathetic results. Meedja is a gimme. A free hit. Just look at websites and write the first thing that comes into your head. Come to the Library and we can Google your first scheme of work. First lesson: Analyse *mise en scène* in Babycat videos.'

For my last lesson with my Set 1s, I asked where they would most like to go on holiday. A boy at the back thrust his arm up in the air and said, 'Bhutan.' I asked why. He said, 'Because it is top of the happiness index. They have no screens. And low pollution. And excellent climate.'

I asked the Set 4s the same question. Milosz stuck his hand up.

'Milosz?'

''Merica.'

'Why?'

'Cos it's sick.'

'Why is it sick?'

''Slebrities.'

I didn't have anything planned for the rest of the lesson, so as a final treat – in addition to the bag of Haribos and cola bottles – I let them write letters to their favourite celebrities. Dear Beyoncé. Dear Kanye. Dear Kim. Dear Wayne. You is the best. Love Me.

I let them read them out. Salim's was wonderful, but he was still too shy to read, so I read it out for him.

Shah Rukh Khan
Delhi

Dear Mr Rukh Khan

I should be typing this but I have to write in my big and good pen I hope this is OK so yeah.

I will like to ask you a couple of questions if I may, my name is Salim and I am 11 years old and live in the UK, If you would kindly tell me how you can become so famous and be in all the cool movies I would watch that all over again more than 15 times. I follow you on Twitter and Instagram so I know that you have a lot of fans. You have 15 million Normal Fans. This leaves 750,000 Crazy Fans. You also have some Hating Fans. I have calculated that you have 150,000 Hating Fans there are 15,000 Hating Fans in Britain 30,000 Hating Fans in America 45,000 Hating Fans in Australia and 60,000 Hating Fans in India. This makes a total of 150,000 Hating Fans.

Don't listen to the Haters. You have inspired me to be a movie star and play in movies even though my parents want me to be a doctor. I want to be like all you people strong, famous and the best of all. When I watch your films I was inspired I would be jumping from the sofa and to the table copying your moves. Any way I am so happy to watch your new film and I will be buying front row seats if I can. My brother was not aloud in cinema until he was only seven. But my dad said he will take me to the cinema in 2 months because he thinks if we spend 25 pounds on popcorn and drinks and the tickets then that is enough for a month or more.

Thank you for reading this letter, and please reply back

Yours faithfully,
Salim

On the last day of the year, there was a cluster of kids hanging around the Department in tears, thunderstruck by the imminent loss of Ho6. Pity the poor buggers – like me – who had to take her classes next year. Ho6 had tried to keep it shtum, but the ads had gone out on the web, so everyone knew.

The final assembly for Ho6 was a deluge of tears, cakes, screeching, hugging, cards, dancing, exhortations of joy and pain. She had been at the school since the Year 13s were in Year 7. She showed photographs of the kids through the years, which prompted great gasps and sighs. As she left, she was mobbed and hugged. Shrieks filled the silent atrium. 'I'm gonna miss you so much'; 'You've meant so much to me'; 'You changed my life.'

The staff gathered in the Canteen to bid farewell to all the leavers. Ho6 read out a selection of letters kids had written her to excuse their late work, laughing through tears.

After sparkling wine, hugs and have-a-great-holidays, I buzzed myself out of the gates for the last time as a New Teacher. From now, I would no longer be the newbie. I was now the Old Guard.

As I walked out of the gates, Donnie ran up to me and thrust a card into my hand. It was a picture of a red-faced man with steam coming out of his ears. In the top right-hand corner it said

IT PARTY TIME!

And inside in bright-red felt-tip:

YOU ARE THE BEST TEACHE
IN THE WORLD EVER!

PART TWO

11

Someone Must Think Something

The 'nice holidays' were nearly over. The world was in clover; my brain was denuded. The smell of Caribbean barbecues and the chirruping of swifts filled the hazy air; all I had done for weeks was sleep, eat and stare at the wall. Occasionally, a thought briefly peeked above the stony earth, only to retreat as swiftly as it had come, fearful of its own growth. One day, Milosz came round to look for his uncle's parrot – he was mortified to realise my house backed onto his – but, apart from that, I had precious little interaction with the human race. It was beautiful.

At the end of August, we went to Thailand with Tom and Kate. Tom and I got drunk and talked about teachers for the first two nights; after that, there was an embargo placed on us discussing school. After a week, I started getting anxious because I hadn't done any preparation for the new term. I kept asking Tom what we were going to teach in Meedja, but he waved it away, saying, 'It will be fine. It will all become clear when we get back. We can't do anything until we have the cameras and the editing equipment anyway.'

I spent the last few days frantically buffing up on my dystopian literature. I skimmed *1984*, *Brave New World*, *Fahrenheit 451*, *Children of Men* and *The Handmaid's Tale*, but I couldn't work out what was dystopian about them. Here were totalitarian regimes, fearful of women, outsiders, intellectuals and books, using surveillance and dumbed-down mass media as means of control. It all seemed pretty realistic. If we swapped the dystopian and non-fiction units, no one would notice.

On the penultimate day, we went to the market in town. As I was buying a fish, I gasped in wonder at how other people lived.

All these people in the world outside of school. All these happy, uniformless children running around playing with sticks and selling fruit, learning how to do things just like that.

'HI, SIRS!!!!!!'

Oh, shit. Yasmin, from Year 10. On holiday with her family. Of course she was.

It was time to go home.

September appeared suddenly, like a child nicking in before me in the queue to take a sponge with custard. There were only a few days to prepare for the new year. I dry-cleaned my suits and replaced the soles on my brogues.

I made a resolution to exercise every day before or after school because I needed some way of keeping the endorphins up, keeping regular, getting the fuckers out of my head, staying sane. The women in the Department went to Zumba or Spin. Tom played five-a-side with the PE lads. Even the MegaDumper found time in his busy schedule dumping to do some rock climbing.

I decided to join the jogging tribe. I downloaded an app that tracked my distance and speed, and then tallied my results against other runners who happen to run that route. When I ran into school the first morning back, awkwardly carrying my clean shirt and suit, I was a wreck by the time I reached Bananaman's shop.

You have run 5.39 miles at an average pace of 8.21 minutes per mile.

I huffed and puffed into the shop. Aisle upon aisle of empty shelves and scattered boxes. It looked like a tornado had ripped through it.

'What happen to you?' asked Bananaman.

'Getting fit,' I said, checking my stats. 'Not bad. Medium quartile. Definitely gonna get into the top quartile by the end of term. I'm all about the Targets now. What happened here?'

'Yah. Terrible. Gonna turn me into another fucking coffee shop.'

'Ah, I'm so sorry.'

'What you gonna do? How those teachers? Why don't you just get fit with some bananaing?'

'I know, I know. I've got it all wrong,' I said as I bought a bag of Haribos. I told him to keep his chin up and sneaked next door for a croissant and a cappuccino.

As I approached the school, I noticed the stately pleasure dome was complete. A shimmering mirage of steel and glass, with not a block of concrete or damp scurf to be found. The school was finished.

I buzzed myself through the gate.

I had to wait ages to get into the toilet to get changed because a holiday in India was playing havoc with MegaDumper's guts. Finally, when I got in, I retched from

153

the pungent smell as I put on my clean shirt, new tie and suit, feeling a sweat patch spread across my back.

The Department had been moved, enlarged, spanked; each work station separated and distant. We shouted across the cold, bright room at each other, telling wistful tales of entire days doing sweet FA on beaches or the sofa. Everyone was tanned and discombobulated, apart from HoD, who was grumbling in the corner, still hungover from an attritional couple of weeks in Suffolk with his ex-wife and daughter.

As I sat down at my computer at 7.43 a.m., I realised I had five lessons that day and no idea what I was going to do. I turned to Tom for help, but he didn't know if he was coming or going. I asked him what the hell I was supposed to be doing for my first Meedja lesson. He waved his hands excitedly in front of my face and said, 'Oh! Yes! I've got just the thing!' He had woken up at 4 a.m., Googled the mark scheme and taken a screenshot of it. I looked at it, but couldn't read it because the writing was so small. After five minutes of squinting, I realised it was the wrong mark scheme. He told me not to worry, that we would work it out, and I should just spend the first few lessons getting them to make films. I asked how they could do that without cameras; he suggested they use their phones; I reminded him they weren't allowed phones in school. He didn't have an answer for this.

'Ah, the Dream Team!' said HoD.

Little Miss Outstanding came over and gave me a chummy punch on the shoulder, and told me all about her holiday in Santorini and how the rest of the time she had 'just chilled out' in Hastings, which seemed unlikely given she had spent it planning the entire unit of dystopian fiction. She sent me the lessons. I clicked on Lesson 1. Grey clouds, neon skyscrapers, flying cars; sunshine, frost, Salvador Dalí melting clocks. 'It was a bright cold day in April and the clocks were striking thirteen.'

In the auditorium, late for INSET, I sat down on a chair like I owned it.

'*Hello, Sir!*' barked VP.

'Hello, Miss!' I said, confidently.

I introduced myself to a new teacher, who looked shit-scared, and was busy filling in her Planner. I picked up my Planner and started casually doodling, as the SMs recited their shtick and Head launched his nukes.

Most of the Department got off lightly, because our results were good. Everyone except HoD. His results would have been perfectly acceptable in the old days – each student had achieved well, each according to their merits – but he hadn't gone the extra mile. He hadn't pushed them into the zone of discomfort.

HoD stood reluctantly, as his results were projected. Half the class was green, the rest orange and red.

'Why did all these students fail to reach their targets?' asked Head.

'They did not "fail",' said HoD, wearily. 'They did fine. More than fine. I'm very happy with them.'

'But they did not reach their targets.'

'No, they did not reach *your* targets. Their marks were overinflated by previous teachers, who were understandably covering their backs, and the target was unrealistic.'

A throat cleared. A chair leg squeaked along the floor.

'What do you mean, "overinflated"?' said Head. 'We all work to the same targets. The same algorithms.'

'And I'm telling you they're unrealistic,' said HoD, walking towards the stage. 'Overinflated. Relentless. Bullshit.'

Head raised his chin. This was pure insubordination, exactly what characterised the *ancien régime*. It had to be stamped out. For it is a fast descent into chaos. Head couldn't wait to get rid of HoD. But he knew that it would be difficult to pull rank because HoD had been at the school longer, and had all the Old Guard onside. Head did not want to make a martyr of HoD, so wisely decided to let the rant burn out.

'This is mindless, inhumane progress for the sake of it,' continued HoD. 'We can't keep getting better and better. We can't; kids can't. Turns out, not all kids are the same. Some kids are better at exams than others. Some year groups are smarter than others. Why are we doing it? Because of the fucking league tables. Because of OFSTED. Not because of wanting the kids to *learn*.'

He turned to face his audience, half of whom gazed at him with admiration, while the other half glared with indignation.

'I cannot think of worse conditions for learning. "You must do this so that this number goes up." "Do this because I need to save my bacon." Because I don't like being made to stand up in front of my colleagues like a skewered bull.'

Head fumed quietly and motioned for HoD to sit down, but HoD hitched up his trousers and began pointing aggressively at the stage.

'When are you going to be happy? When you get eighty per cent? Ninety per cent? A hundred per cent? What will you do when every pupil in the school gets a hundred per cent A*s? Where will you have to go then?'

'Sit. Down.'

HoD slowly returned to his seat, like a recalcitrant Year 9, still swearing under his breath.

My Year 12 form arrived in dribs and drabs around 8.29 a.m. the next day. A series of disarmingly well-dressed young men and women, of every hue, complexion and hair gradation, who looked like they were going for an interview at a blue-chip firm, stopped in the doorway. I greeted them with a smile. They grunted, wandered to a computer, dropped their bags on the floor with a thud, turned on the computer and collapsed behind the screen.

A particularly sluggish boy called Liam started giggling when I chastised him for turning on his computer.

'Liam, is it?' I said.

'Yeah, sir.'

'We have to spend the next year together. We need to do a deal. If you get in on time, I'll give you excellent references. You scratch my back, I scratch yours.'

'A'right, Sir.'

'OK. Now. Onwards. I hope you've had a good break. I can see by your tans that some of you have had a great holiday. But can I urge you to come down from your Goa high as quickly as you can. This is, after all, the most crucial year in your school career. You can't wait until January to get started, not like Man U . . .'

A couple of muffled grunts. I clearly had to raise my bantz for sixth formers.

A boy entered, muttering, 'Sorryi'mlate.' He looked like a refugee from the late nineties: his long lank hair was in a ponytail, which reached the collar of his long black trenchcoat. He clumped to his desk in his black DM boots, and dumped his low-slung Tippexed bag on the desk. Many things were immediately clear: he hadn't washed his hair in weeks; he had gone to private school; his parents were sending him here to game the system and get him into Oxbridge; his anarchic pose was thinly veiled – underneath, he just needed to be loved.

'I take it the Head of Sixth Form took issue with your hair,' I said.

'Yeah. It's a fucking disgrace. Sorry. A disgrace.'

'And your coat.'

'What's wrong with it? The teachers think I'm a teacher!'

'Great. Well, you can take the register then. You're Walter, I take it?'

'Wally. Call me Wally.'

'Wally.'

'Mate –'

'Sir.'

'Sir. Can you call the technicians? My screen doesn't work.'

As I walked over to try and help him, I noticed everyone was on Facebook.

'OK, so let's just set a few ground rules, yes?' I said. 'Form time is for working and discussing and stimulating our minds. I don't want to see you on social media. In fact, I don't want to see you on computers at all.'

They stared at me, then stared back at their screens.

'Fine. Tune out. See if I care.' I sat down at my desk in a huff. 'Is this how you are going to behave in your university interview? Is it? Do you think anyone is going to let you into their university if you just sit there like an amoeba? Seriously. These precious few minutes we have together before school each day are the only time you have to prepare for university. Imagine I am an admissions tutor. So, Liam: why do you want to come to this university?'

Liam made a triangle with his fingers.

'I think you may be in the wrong place,' I said. 'You seem to be applying to *Play School*?'

'Nah, Sir. I was watching this thing on YouTube yeah about Jay Z yeah –'

'Please stop now.'

'No, Sir, you dunno what I'm gonna say –'

'I do. I really do.'

'Yeah so basically right the world yeah is run by –'

''Luminati?'

I made a triangle shape with my hands.

Liam leapt to his feet, and spun round and around, gripping his cheeks with one hand and pointing at me with the other.

'No. Way! No. Way! Sir knows! SIR KNOWS!!!!!'

Lesson #175

Top Behaviour Management Tip:
If You Go up to Any Kid, Make a Triangle
Sign with Your Hands and Say, ''Luminati',
You Will Have Omnipotent Control.

'Luminati – or 'The Illuminati' – is a Theory of Everything invoked by every crackpot and lunatic on the internet and therefore is received wisdom for the kids. I have sat through presentations from classes in every year group on this very topic, and they all swear down that 'Luminati are, for good or ill, the governing cosmology.

'OK,' I said, preparing to engage with the madness. 'Imagine I'm from the Planet Zog. What, pray, are "'Luminati"?'

'All right, Sir, but if you are from Planet Zog, then chances are you have met 'Luminati,' said Liam, tapping his forehead.

'We're off to a flying start.'

'So, the 'Luminati, yeah, are actually these massive worms, yeah, from space, yeah, who wear human-being overcoats. And what they do, yeah, is come down and then start running tings.'

'I see. Sounds scary.'

'True say. It is dat. So, like, everyone in power, yeah' – he registered my look of scorn – 'or like *most* people in power, are 'Luminati. They are all in the triangle.'

He made the triangle with his hands. I made the triangle with my hands. Everyone went 'Ooooooooh!!!!'

'Like the one on the dollar bill?' I enquired.

'*Zackly*. The All-Seeing Eye in the pyramid! Yeah. Dat's 'Luminati. 'Luminati run every fing. Banks. Hollywood. 9/11.'

I told him this was sounding anti-Semitic, but was shouted down as others joined in with their nominations: David Cameron, Jay Z, Prince Philip, Tony Blair,

Justin Bieber. I admitted that it was, in fact, a fairly broad church.

'Just look at this school!' Liam said, pointing out of the window.

'Triangles everywhere! The playground! The chimneys! The logos! The All-Seeing Eye is everywhere. They see every fing you do.'

Hmm. Maybe he's onto something.

'So let me get this straight,' I said. 'You think the world is run by lizards?'

'True say. It's a 'spiracy.'

'Innit! 'Spiracy!'

'Well, Liam, I would like to welcome you to our august institution.'

'So, you gonna let me go Oxford now?'

'No!'

'Please! Lemme go Oxford.'

'I'll let you go as soon as you learn to use the definite article.'

The bell went.

'I'll see you later for English.'

'Bye, Sir.'

'Bye, Liam.'

'Safe, Sir.'

'Formal language, please.'

'Yeah, safe.'

'And take that earring out before the Head of Sixth Form sees it.'

'Yeah, whatevs.'

'*Au revoir, les enfants.*'

I had a couple of minutes before my first lesson, so I returned to the Department, poured a cup of coffee and ate a croissant. HoD was looking out the window, chuckling to himself. I asked what he was laughing at, and he beckoned me over.

'Come look at this. This is better than Jason fucking Bourne.'

I joined him and watched the playground for a while. Nothing much seemed to be happening. Just happy kids reuniting.

'What am I looking at?'

'There. See that woman there? Long white hair? Floaty dress?'

'Yeah. Who's she?'

'New Head of Sixth Form.'

'OK. So?'

'Now look around. What else do you see?'

Head was circling a few feet away from her.

'Head.'

'Anyone else? Look closely.'

A few feet beyond Head was another SM, watching and talking on his walkie-talkie. Above him, leaning out of a classroom window, was another SM, talking on her walkie-talkie. Scanning across the school, I saw two more SMs, scrutinising Ho6's every move, then talking into their walkie-talkies.

'Where are the sniper guns?' I asked.

'Exactly. What the hell are they saying to each other? That kid is running and she didn't stop him! She just walked past a sweet wrapper! Take her out!'

'Where has she come from?'

'Dunno. Somewhere far too relaxed. Just look at her. Woah, man! Hippy, hippy shake! Way too floaty. I give her until the end of the week.'

PERIOD 1: *THE TRUMAN SHOW* WITH YEAR 9 SET 4

Starter: 'Can you imagine what it is like to be watched the whole time?'

'Er . . . YEAH?!'

'What if your whole life was a story being written by someone else?'

'Say what?'

'Woooah.'

I put up a slide with Plato's bust and a picture of a cave. I said that what they thought was reality was a delusion; we were all just watching shadows on the wall of the cave.

'Wooaah.'

I told them not to worry, because I was going to lead them out into the light of truth. They looked at me askance, like they had short-circuited; after a long silence, they said they missed Miss.

PERIOD 2: *HAMLET*, YEAR 8 SET 3

Wow.

7s had become 8s.

What a difference a summer makes. It was like watching one of those David Attenborough documentaries, in which the editors speed up images of a plant taken across a year, so it seems as if it has grown in seconds. It was terrifying to behold. Their features had been mutated and stretched in strange and unflattering ways: elongated heads, dropped voices, massive hands. Half of my old class stayed in Set 4, to be drilled into shape by VP, who they were petrified of. Donnie, Saadia and Mercedes came up to Set 3, which was good for me, because we had established a relationship. Becoming established is half the battle.

I asked Saadia how her summer was. She said fine and sat down at the front.

Well, that's the only word I'm going to get out of her this year.

Donnie's evolution into a swot continued apace. When he walked in that first lesson wearing glasses, carrying a briefcase, and plopped himself down under my nose, I didn't recognise him. I asked him how his summer was. He told me proudly how many books he had read – *The Hunger Games* (all of them), *Diary of a Wimpy Kid* (all of them), Harry Potter (most of them) – so I told him to give book reviews every week, which he duly did, staying behind every day to write them.

Mercedes was growing out of her chubby awkwardness to develop into a confident girl. She came in and waved at me vigorously, as if she was on a ship returning to dock, growling, 'HI, SIR! IT'S ME! DID YOU MISS ME?' I told her that there were times, on that beach in Thailand, when I thought, 'I really wish Mercedes was here.' That was a good icebreaker. The rest of the class went 'Oooohhhh!' and 'Naaahhhhh!' and 'Siiirrr's baaaaddd!' I told them all to be quiet and that the next person who made a noise was in detention. I held them there for a long time in silence, as I went through the register, and grilled each of them about their deportment, and how whatever they were doing may have been what they did with Sir or Miss last year, but if they thought they were going to get away with that *this* year, they had another thing coming. Then we looked at the opening of *Hamlet*. I turned the lights off and we all made spooky ghost sounds and created a world of uncertainty and fear. I flashed a torch in their eyes suddenly and shouted, 'Who's there?' They were terrified, in hysterics.

At break, I had to set up my lesson for Year 12.

At last! The Elysian Fields of Sixth Form. The sweet spot when a book really hits you. The book your English teacher tells you to read, and it changes the course of your life forever. I had to introduce them to A Level Literature, sure, but more importantly, to the literature that would balm their souls for the rest of their lives.

We couldn't be dealing with stratified rows for such an open forum, so I put the desks in horseshoe formation. It looked a bit like a corporate brainstorming session, but once I got the poetry and music going, it would be totally different. My first lesson was going to be like a cross between an eighteenth-century salon and a beatnik happening.

I put verses of poetry on the walls (Blake, Langston Hughes, Rilke, Carol Ann Duffy, e e cummings), some Modernist art (*The Scream*, *Les Demoiselles d'Avignon*, Duchamp's *Urinal*), and a series of portraits (Yeats, Charlotte Brontë, Jean Rhys, Arundhati Roy, Miles Davis, James Baldwin). I played an album of Beat Poetry. I remembered that I had to put a bit of British Values into my English lessons, so I stuck Shakespeare and Milton back up (they were languishing in a plastic bin full of old exams) and surrounded the room with Union Jack bunting, but that just made it look like a Rotary Club, so I took it down again. I placed a Bramley Apple Pie on each desk and waited.

PERIOD 3: INTRODUCTION TO A LEVEL, YEAR 12

One by one, they gingerly entered and stood with their backs to me.

'Come in! Come in! Welcome to our salon! Make yourself comfortable. Find a chair. Or beanbag. And chill out.'

They were completely freaked out. Their entire school career they had been told to be quiet and write in silence. Who was this freak?

'Just sit down! Sit down wherever. And read some poetry! Yeah! Whenever you feel like it!'

Gradually, they sat and stared at the poems. They seemed distracted by Jack Kerouac talking bollocks in the background.

'OK, guys!' I said, chummily. 'So who wants to go first? Who has read any of these poems before?'

Alexia put her hand up.

'OK, cool! That's cool! So where did you read it?'

'At home.'

'Cool. Nice. And what do you think of it?'

'It's good. Yup. I like it.'

'OK. Anyone else have anything to say about the poems that they are looking at?'

Post-nuclear-fallout silence.

'No? OK. Why don't you swap poems?'

Five minutes passed. A beatnik with a heavy New York accent recited a poem about a telephone being stuck to his head.

'Anyone?' I asked, frustrated. 'Someone must think something.'

You would have thought.

They didn't peep. I rationalised that they were not used to each other yet. Still stuck in Year 11 self-consciousness. I asked what their favourite books were. Nobody said anything. Eventually Alexia said *The Bell Jar* and Zainab said *Things Fall Apart*, but they were too shy to say why they liked them. Isaac said he liked graphic novels. Ella couldn't think of anything.

'Come on! You must be able to think of something!' I implored.

She shrugged. 'Wassat one? Wiv da big dumb guy and da little one?'

'*Of Mice and Men*?'

'Yeah. Dat.'

'OK. Any others?'

'*Macbef*?'

'Any you haven't done for GCSE?'

She shook her head.

I scanned over the class list, and saw that Ella had been awarded a C at GCSE.

'Well, why are you doing English A Level?'

'Dunno. Goes well wiv Meedja. And I had Miss. I liked Miss.'

A chorus of 'Yeah. We loved Miss.'

The Beat Poetry album finished with a jazz musician poet tapping out a beat on a drum, crying, 'BROOKS BROTHERS, MARX BROTHERS, MY BROTHERS, WHEN WILL YOU CRY LIFE'S SWEET SONG?'

I was drowning. Time to move on, swiftly. Bring the purpose back. I turned the computer on and opened the first dystopia lesson.

On the board were images of a gas mask, cloned sheep, a freeze frame of Ethan Hawke and Uma Thurman in *Gattaca*, book burning, a futuristic cityscape with flying cars and terrible pollution, Big Brother, and Thomas More's island of utopia with a red line through it.

'What are we doing this term?' I asked.

'Biology?'

'The Future?'

'Close. What kind of future?'

'Dystopias.'

'Good.'

I clicked on to a quote, in black Garamond on a white background:

> **A book is a loaded gun in the house next door.**
> **Burn it. Take the shot from the weapon.**
> **Breach man's mind.**
> **— *Fahrenheit 451***

'Who's read this?'

Alexia, Zainab and Isaac put up their hands.

'You should have all read it over the holidays . . .'

Liam was nodding vigorously.

'What was your favourite book that you read, Liam?'

'Ah . . . that's difficult to say, Sir. Yeah. Difficult.'

'Because you didn't read any of them?'

'Nah, nah. I read them. I just . . .'

'Forgot them?'

'Nah. I'm just still . . . finking about dem, Sir.'

'All right, Liam. You have until the end of the week.'

I clicked onto my final slide. A pile of books and a bunch of flowers.

'For the Plenary: what is the significance of this?'

They shook their heads as they walked out.

I slumped back in my chair.

Next lesson, I should aptually electrocute them.

PERIOD 4: *A VIEW FROM THE BRIDGE*, YEAR 11 SET 3

After the usual complaints that they wanted to have Miss, I jumped straight into the context. We began with the same slide I used for *Jason and the Argonauts* and *Holes*: what does it feel like to leave home? What does it feel like to arrive somewhere different? What does it feel like to be an outsider?

We watched a documentary about Ellis Island; we created an Ellis Island in the classroom and imagined we were arriving there for the first time. We practised terrible *Bwooklin* accents, and role-played the conversation we would have with the immigration officials. We imagined the bridge was over a river in our town and we wrote a story about immigrant communities who lived there. I told them we were just going to read the play and not stress, because they had enough of that to deal with later in the year. They were warming to me.

Lunch. Walked over to the Canteen with Little Miss Outstanding and Tom. Didn't even think about bolting for the graveyard. Lasagne. Get in. Tom psyched me up for Meedja, and said I just needed to do a simple introduction lesson in which I asked them what they had seen and maybe find some good clips of old films like *Le Voyage dans la lune*. I could stretch that out over an hour, no problem.

PERIOD 5: MEEDJA, YEAR 12

Worse than I could have ever feared. I asked, 'What have you seen?' We sat in silence for most of the lesson. Eventually I asked Ella, 'Why are you doing Media?'

She shrugged and said, 'Goes well wiv English.'

'Why are any of you doing Media?' I asked.

Shrugs.

'Like social media.'

'Yeah.'

'Everyfing's Media.'

PERIOD 6: MEEDJA, YEAR 12

I put on *Le Voyage dans la lune* and asked what they thought of it.

Shrugs.

'Ella?'

'Bare old.'

'Why do you say that?'

'Black and white.'

'Anything else?'

'Bare boring.'

'Why?'

'Black and white.'

'Anything else?'

'French. Gave up French.'

'But there were subtitles.'

'Gave up reading.'

I put on *The Truman Show* and told them about Plato's cave. They went 'Wooah' and looked at me funny.

At the end of the day, I went back to the Department and wrote an email to HoD, cc'ing Tom.

```
I know the term has technically begun, but
I am pleading with you to make a change to
my timetable.


I don't want to teach Media
I don't want to teach Media
I don't want to teach Media
I would quite like to teach History
Or anything else
Except Media
```

Tom came in and looked over my shoulder.

'I take it the first lesson didn't go so well.'

'I don't care what you have to do, but just get me out of this.'

HoD walked in.

'What did you do to Ella?'

'Nothing. Why?'

'She came to see me in tears at lunchtime. Said she wanted to change from English and Meedja to just Meedja. Then she came to see me just now in even more tears saying she wants to drop Meedja too. You sadistic tyrant! What did you do to her?'

'I asked her what she had read. Then I asked her what she had seen.'

'That'll do it.'

Suddenly, Little Miss Outstanding burst into the Department in floods of tears. I put my arm around her and asked what was wrong. She said that all the boys in her new Year 11 class had been bullying her. I sat her down and made her a tea. Through shuddering sobs she said that she had posted pictures of herself on Facebook in a bikini on holiday in Santorini and that all the boys had seen it.

Who'd have thought it? You put up risqué photos of yourself onto a giant noticeboard which billions of people have access to, and then *Boom!* Your pervy pupils go and look at it.

I told her not to worry, and rushed off to Debating Club.

We all had new responsibilities this year. Little Miss Outstanding was now editing the school magazine. Tom was granted his Chutney Club on the roof of the Science block. I got Debating Club.

There used to be a module at GCSE called Speaking and Listening, which our kids flourished at because they are often much better at telling stories than writing them and are so damn funny and their stories so extraordinary. But the government abolished Speaking and Listening at GCSE. They are the two least rigorous senses, after all.

PERIOD 7: DEBATING CLUB

I started with a lesson from the system, which featured a balloon debate in which the kids had to decide whether to throw Wayne Rooney, Justin Bieber, 50 Cent or Britney Spears out of a balloon. They became extremely animated by this, and passionately defended their lumpen celebrity of choice.

I fired them up with arch interjections, like 'I am amazed the balloon can get off the ground at all, given the weight of jewellery and egos involved.'

They said, 'Ooooooh, Sir! Nah, Sir! You're baaaaaaad. You're well out of order!'

I assured them that as an avid Belieber, we were going to keep Justin safe, no matter what.

To help them, I showed them examples of debates on *Question Time* and BBC Parliament to model how to debate issues. About halfway through, a kid asked why these posh people weren't put in detention for shouting out, interrupting each other and name calling. I realised that political discourse had become so toxic that I could no longer find suitable examples to show them. The world was regressing, becoming more primitive. In this new Looking Glass world, the adults in power were behaving worse than Year 7 Set 4s. Don't copy the adults, kids. Keep the outside out.

That afternoon we did euthanasia. I had the video primed. This one couldn't fail. It was BBC, after all. And it had Terry Pratchett in it, so there was some cultural enrichment in there too. I watched the film over and over to check there was nothing unsuitable. I followed best practice by checking with Mentor that there was no one in the class who might react badly to the issue. The film showed an elderly couple travelling to Dignitas in Switzerland so that the husband can bring an end to the misery of his incurable illness. They are paragons of dignity. After he calmly slips away, she turns and stands, unruffled, looking out of the frosted window at the deep snow. British values in full effect.

The kids dealt with it with great maturity and sensitivity. I was destroyed by it, wiping tears from my eyes. Here I was, their teacher, the one who was supposed to be revealing the mysteries of life to them, but I was teaching something I knew nothing about.

12

Emily

I am very worried about her. She is always wan, withdrawn. She definitely isn't well. I think she stays up all night. It's impossible to pin down exactly what the problem is. Anorexia? Bulimia? Someone said she might be epileptic. I should call home, but I believe all her family have now passed.

It may just be shyness. She is terribly, terribly shy and introverted. She can barely look me in the eye. Always quiet. Hates to be asked questions. Incredibly evasive and prickly.

It's probably just depression. Well, melancholy. The more antique disposition. A natural by-product of her astonishing intelligence. My God, is she bright. She knows it all. When she does choose to speak, the rest of the class is silent, while we digest what she has said. And it will be, invariably, the most surprising and original thing I have heard all week. She is sharp, blasphemous, outrageous, iconoclastic, defiantly feminist, hilarious. And then she leaves us there, dangling –

While we struggle to keep up.

But she is utterly confounding. One minute she is warm and winsome, almost coquettish – yes, flirtatious – while she shares her most intimate thoughts with me late into the night. And then, just as I think I have got her onside, she turns on me with savage glee. She can be truly unsettling; definitely the most disturbing person I have taught. But she is also the most exciting discovery I have made. Yet almost impossible to teach.

I am regularly struck dumb when trying to teach her. Like Billy Collins, I want to lift her 'tippet made of tulle' from her shoulders and lay it on the back of the chair, to untie her bonnet, so her hair unfurls, to fiddle with the tiny mother-of-pearl buttons down the back of her long white dress . . .

That's right. I have fallen in love with Emily Dickinson.

Every lesson we did something different. The first lesson we just looked at that haunting daguerreotype, one of the only images of her in existence. We know so little about Emily. And that is why she is great to teach. We need that distance, that space to discover.

We tried to imagine her life. I gave them a bit of context from Emerson and the Transcendentalists. Liam liked Emerson's quote about how he was a 'transparent eyeball'; he said, 'Oooh', and made the triangle with his hands.

We walked around the room, turning on each beat, so even if the line didn't make explicit sense, at least they embodied the rhythm. It was the same principle as teaching Shakespeare – establish the iambic heartbeat, and you understand it. Liam was very gifted at drama, so he directed a dramatisation of 'I felt a Funeral, in my Brain', where the whole class was standing around the grave, singing the chorus as a gospel choir. Alexia was a fabulous creative writer, so we often wrote imaginary

letters to Emily from her lovers, based on the fragments
of poetry found on envelopes that had once contained
lost letters. We imagined which words were cut when her
poems were edited, instead of all those damn hyphens.
We even created her Facebook page. She didn't have
many friends, sadly.

We all found different things in the poems. Wally thought they were about one thing, and one thing
only. He didn't do ambiguity. I remember when we did
Antony and Cleopatra at school, my English teacher said,
'Everyone is either a Roman or an Egyptian.' Wally was
a Roman, for whom every line was a straight road to a
place he already knew. For Wally, Emily was a chick stuck
in her attic who needed to get out more and get some.
Every poem was about sex, or lack thereof. All literature
was. That was why he was doing it for A Level. Zainab
and Alexia began challenging him on his sexism, but he
reacted by 'calling the Politically Correct police'. He was
just saying what everyone else was thinking, after all.
Although if he thought he was going to get laid, he had a
funny way of going about it. He was happy to discourse
about his use of porn, which made all the girls in the class
retch. I tried to pander to his basest instincts by telling
them to put on 'their filth goggles' when reading 'A Narrow Fellow in the Grass', which really does have a sexual
dimension. Wally sniggered like Finbarr Saunders all the
way through, but the rest of them didn't buy it. Zainab
said, 'Isn't it just about a snake in the grass?'

'Is that would you would prefer?' I asked.

'Yes!' she said.

I concurred that maybe it was just about a snake in the grass. But they couldn't just say that in the exam. What else?

Zainab was also a Roman – she could only see God. She saw no struggle, no conflict. The Narrow Fellow was Jesus. That was that.

Alexia was an Egyptian with a fertile imagination, who led us deftly towards a richer understanding of the poem. For her, it was just about nature, transcendentalism, the end of innocence, androgyny, and a radical rejection of Emily's role within an overbearing patriarchal society.

Ella thought whatever Alexia thought.

The glorious thing was that we could not have a final, definitive answer. No categorical tick or cross. The opacity and mystery of her poetry kept us intrigued, and, in the deathless phrase of a thousand kids, 'made us want to read on'.

And read it again.

13

The Letting Go

At the end of another long, attritional, baffling and exult-ant day, I walked into the Department and was confronted by a weird guy in my chair. He wasn't just in my chair. He was *tipping backwards on it*.

I exited fast, and observed him. Tom approached to find me crouched down with my nose pressed against the glass.

'Who the hell is that?' I whispered.

'New Trainee,' said Tom. 'But he's not going to last long with that kind of chair etiquette. Ponce alert.'

'Who's training him?'

'You are.'

'Fuck off.'

'What? You're ready. I believe in you.'

'Oh, seriously. Go fuck yourself.'

'What's the problem? He's taking your Year 8s off you. You just have to sit there.'

'Ah. Good point.'

'I'll do it if you want –'

'No, no. He's mine!'

We watched him as he read from a book, and ran his fingers through his long wavy hair. Suddenly he leapt up and walked around the Department, talking to himself animatedly. He stopped before the window and pointed at an unsuspecting girl in the playground, shouting, 'GET THEE TO A NUNNERY!'

Oh God. Every trainer's nightmare. A Frustrated Actor.

Tom and I went in and introduced ourselves.

'Rehearsing?' I asked.

'Sorry. Yes. Just practising for tomorrow. It really is one of the most challenging scenes to perfect.'

'Yes. You do realise your audience will be Year 8 Set 3?'

'Ah. Marvellous. Perhaps you might offer me some direction . . .?'

'You know that it's a lesson? In which you have to teach?'

He arched an eyebrow. He clearly didn't.

I came home that evening to find Amy standing in the hallway holding a stick. We hugged and kissed and danced around the kitchen.

At last.

A child.

Who is not someone else's.

I was nervous about telling people at work, but no one seemed very surprised.

Everyone was very kind. Genuinely excited, even. It felt like telling family. They already started suggesting names: William. John. Ernest. F. Scott. Daisy. Emily. Chinua. Mercedes. Chika. Salim. Milosz.

Mentor sent an image of Virgin and Child, with my face superimposed over the Virgin and the Child.

I thought about telling my classes. But I didn't want the 11s or 12s to think I was abandoning them just before their exams. And I knew the 8s and 9s would all go 'UURG-GGHHHH!' or 'AHHHHH!' and generally create a massive distraction, and think that I was having the baby with Little Miss Outstanding (there were only so many adults in the world, after all, and they were all in the school; if you ate lunch with another teacher, you were going to have babies with them).

During Staff Briefing, Head showed us pictures of British officers cooking breakfast for their men in Afghanistan. 'What does this picture say to you?' he said. Mick shouted, 'HUNGRY.' Head made it clear that this was deadly serious. 'It says three things to me,' he said. 'Number 1: Teamwork. Number 2: No 'I' in TEAM. Number 3: Morale boost.'

That Saturday, he made all the staff come to school for a 'British Breakfast'. I arrived just as his black BMW with the tinted windows glided through the gates, and watched him as he walked into the Canteen. He came back out a few minutes later wearing a chef's apron and hat. I followed him up to the DT Department.

'Come in! Make yourself comfortable!' he instructed, as he beat some eggs. A Muslim SM was frying the bacon.

After half an hour, we were sitting in a room full of smoke from burnt toast and sausages, making polite conversation, sipping orange juice, trying to suppress coughs. I was desperate to get home, do my marking, look after Amy.

After we had eaten breakfast and cleared up, it was nearly lunchtime. I found a moment when he was eating alone to tell him my news.

'How did this happen?' he asked.

'Erm . . .'

I thought about inviting him to my Sex Ed class. I was a pro now.

Lesson #182:
Teaching Sex Ed Is Easy.

I was really apprehensive about showing Year 9s how to put a condom on, but in the end, it was the easiest lesson of the year. I followed the Science teacher's technique: rest it on top of the dildo 'like a sombrero', and then unfurl straight down in one easy motion. They were so unnerved. Even the tough boys didn't dare try, for fear of not being able to do it.

'I mean: how long have you known about this?' asked Head.

'Erm . . . not long,' I stuttered. 'But don't worry. It won't clash with exams.'

'Good.' He grumpily finished eating his banger and handed out greasy feedback forms for us to fill in.

How do you think the British Breakfast went?
Which British Values did you identify before, during or after the British Breakfast?
How can you incorporate elements of the British Breakfast into your own teaching practice?

It was all going to be fine. Fine. What could go wrong? Miller was going great; we'd read the play, lifted chairs in varying levels of machismo, done the Trial of Marco with the whole class as a jury, and the most voluble kids as attorneys; now all they needed to do was loads of practice in unseen poetry and comprehensions based on newspaper articles; the 12s were all over Dickinson; the 9s, I could just show *The Truman Show* every lesson; Meedja, slap on YouTube; the 8s were being taken over by Trainee, so I didn't have to do any planning or marking. Just sit there and enjoy some amateur dramatics.

But Trainee turned out to be a lot of work. It's all very well being able to recite a speech or direct a scene and talk about character motivation and all that, but you *aptually* have to teach them things these days. And he really didn't get that.

Just before his first lesson, I asked him if he would like to take a break from swinging back on my chair to take a look at the lesson he was about to deliver. He said he was fine and that he needed to do his breathing exercises. He was lying on the floor, saying, 'Inhale Pink, Exhale Blue!' when HoD entered. HoD mouthed, 'He's getting your job', and walked out again.

I had told the Year 8s that they were going to get a new teacher for a while. They were cool with that. But I don't think they were prepared for what was coming.

Trainee entered the classroom with his trousers tucked into his socks, wearing a beret and carrying a small plastic sword. They pissed themselves. When he finally regained control, he made Mercedes read Ophelia (we hadn't got very far in six weeks).

Lesson #199:
You Never Get Through The Text.
You Rarely Get Halfway.

Mercedes stumbled her way through as best she could, stifling giggles.

> My lord, as I was sewing in my closet,
> Lord Hamlet, with his doublet all unbraced;
> No hat upon his head; his stockings fouled,
> Ungartered –

'HAHAHAPLEASESIRSOZZLESQUAZZLESCAN'T DOIT!!!!'

Trainee was acting it all out. He undid his blazer, tossed his beret aside, pushed his socks down, and dropped to his knee before her. I had a flashback to the pomegranate. No way back.

As I watched him, I realised that training to be a teacher was like being a terrible actor stuck in a matinee performance, and never feeling comfortable in your role. The audience titter and smirk at you and then walk out. And then you have to go see the theatre director for notes. What was I supposed to say? 'Darling, you were MAHvellous. The way you dealt with that heckler. Well, all of them. Don't worry about hoi polloi. I was rapt, utterly rapt . . .'

At the end of the lesson, I patted him on the back and said, 'Great, let's catch up later.' I ran out of the lesson to get away from the throng who wanted their practice papers back – which I still had not marked – out into the playground, waved at Salim, gave Donnie a friendly tap on the shoulder, and came to a standstill at precisely 10 a.m., where I acknowledged the Duty Manager with a salute, put my hands behind my back, and adopted my stern duty face.

Skip. Skip. Skip. Skip. Skip.

I looked up at the clock. I had five minutes. Enough time to check my phone. I reached into my pocket.

Text message.

From my mother.

Please ring asap.

I knew exactly what that meant.

The outside was about to come crashing in.

Dad had died.

I don't remember much after that. I found Mentor, who organised for my lessons to be covered that afternoon. I left in a daze and found my way home to the car and then I drove, I don't know how, guided by some reptilian GPS. My mother was sitting at the table, head in hands. We hugged and cried. I said, 'What are you going to do?' And immediately felt like an idiot. She said, 'It's only been a few hours.'

I had to do something, so after lots of tea and staring, I went to the Funeral Director's, which was at the corner of a busy crossroads, nestled between the police station, a mosque, a bank, Mothercare and a Poundshop.

One of that lot has to protect him.

The woman behind the counter of the Funeral Director's was jolly and welcoming. I said my father was in there. She looked at me, smiled, and then said, 'Oh, yeah! Dead ringer!'

I stared at her.

Surely your only job is *not* to say something like that.

'Oh, sorry! I didn't mean . . .'

Standing outside in the cold wind as people bustled by with bags overflowing with Poundshop bargains, I felt the loneliness of this first night dead. For after tonight, nothing would ever be different.

I walked home breathing deep, gusty air. I looked up at the moon's broken glare through the branches of the trees. *I am alive.*

But when I woke the next day, I could not get up. I tried to deny reality. I kept trying to go back to sleep and wake up different. But I only got more tired, more blotchy, more dazed. For a week, it was just dark, dark, dark.

I spent the whole week in my dressing-gown trying to find a poem to read at the funeral. I must have gone through every single poem in the canon. Most poems I had to read three or four times, partly because they were incomprehensible, but partly because all I had been conditioned to do was spot shit like alliteration and sibilance. I suddenly realised I couldn't read poetry. What does any of this stuff *aptually* mean? A lifetime of literature, and all you care about is the literature, not the life. Like that guy in *The English Patient* who says, 'It comes from having read too much into too little.'

Dad would want *The Four Quartets*.

Of course he would.

That was how he communicated with me, so that is how I would make my final communication with him.

The day burned bright, the sun flaming the dew on the tombstones of the secluded chapel, as I read words from *The Four Quartets* that sounded like they had been written especially for this day.

History was now and England.

At home, we played Leonard Cohen loud. I stood by the mantelpiece and looked at pictures of myself as a baby being held by my father, and I felt a profound sense of time collapsing.

Time present was time past was time future.

Tick. Excellent. Check tense.

Gradually, staff found out and offered condolences.

Thanks, yeah, terrible, thanks.

I really didn't want the kids to find out. I had spent the last year erecting this carapace of strength, this impregnable persona, and now it was going to be totally undermined. But they smell you out.

A day or two later, while waiting for Trainee to appear from behind the Dry Erase Retractable Whiteboard/arras, Mercedes said, 'Are you sad, Sir?' I paused. 'Yes. Yes, Mercedes, I am.' And she said, 'Sorry.' I thanked her, like a dear friend. 'We miss you,' she whispered. 'I miss you too,' I said.

Head didn't say a word. Nothing. Not one word. Every time he walked past me, he just blanked me.

Howl, howl, howl! O, you are men of stones!

One day an SM came up to me by the photocopier, put an arm around me and said, 'I am very sorry.' It turned out that she had lost her father the year before. They weren't all autobots after all.

She said, 'You're just numb, aren't you?'

Numb.

Yes, numb.

That's it.

Exactly.

Numb.

And numb was the way forward. I had to numb myself with beeps and grind, with exam prep and data input. The only response to fathomless pain.

And it worked. I learned to love the numb quotidian grind.

Just keep numbing it out.

Everything was structured. Routine. Steady. Settled. I planned. Delivered. Marked. Fedback. Planned. Delivered. Marked. Fedback. I didn't have to think. I clocked in and clocked out.

Bell goes.

Ding!

Slobber.

Answers.

Ariel. 18 point.

Practice Papers for the 11s, 12s and 13s.

Wag wag wag.

Hineni. Here I am. God. Here I am.

Just keeping it numb.

I had to make revision booklets for the mocks. The Emily Dickinson booklets were particularly numbing, because I mindlessly went on the internet and copied and pasted the poetry from any old website, but it turned out that it was the wrong version, so I had to go through and change every hyphen into an en-dash. And that's a lot of hyphens.

After great pain -

No, like that –

Exactly.

Numb –

Amy and I had booked to go to Iceland over Christmas. I said I wasn't sure if it was a good idea now, but Amy insisted. What had been intended as a purifying escape now looked like it was going to be a pure reflection of my emotional state. I had spent over a year listening to Little Miss Outstanding bang on about Pathetic Fallacy; now I was *aptually* going to experience it. On the plane, I listened to *The Letting Go* by Bonnie 'Prince' Billy, which he recorded in Iceland, and thought about *Brave New World*. Here I am, God. An Epsilon in exile. Obi-Wan banished to the mountains of Tatooine.

The hotel was wedged between a sheer glacier and a green, broiling sea. A solitary black church stood on the headland. We walked along the black volcanic beach, as a hurricane whipped up around us. Amy tried to talk to me, but I couldn't hear her over the wind. That afternoon, we went to a water park and I got stuck at the top of a waterslide in the howling gale. We drove back, through the eye of the storm, with the car lifting off the road. All I could see was tumult and chaos.

When we got back to the hotel, we sat quietly and stared at the crashing waves. A Physics teacher from my school walked in with his girlfriend. I greeted him like a long-lost brother. We discussed all the people who were leaving the school; how sad it was; how it wasn't going to be the same. I said at least we were still holding out, but then he admitted that he too was leaving. I expressed all the sadness and shock I was capable of, which wasn't much given the circumstances, and asked why. He gave the boilerplate reasons – done my time, too much red tape, got stale, just want to be allowed to teach, love the kids but had enough of SM, don't want to be an SM, time to shit or get off the pot – before sheepishly admitting he was going to a private school.

We stared at the sea some more, weighed down by immensity. Finally, I was feeling something. Finally, I was thinking about something. I realised that this was the first time I had thought about anything for years. I was paid to think, and to help children think, and yet I spent most of my time chasing my tail in a frantic muddle. I felt time collapse into an eternal present. I could finally approach my grief, and became very upset thinking about how my father would not get to meet his grandson. Amy comforted me by telling me that I could honour his memory by being such a father to my son. To become a real father is to become a real son. There was a torch that was being passed on, like that from teacher to pupil. I pledged to her that, whatever else happened, all I wanted to be was a proper father to my child.

I lay awake in the endless dusk reading Emily.

> This is the Hour of Lead –
> Remembered, if outlived,
> As Freezing persons, recollect the Snow –
> First – Chill – then Stupor – then the letting go –

14

Personality Recalled

Tuesday, Period 6. The Hour of Lead. The weekend has yet to heave into view. Lunch rush is over. Blood sugar is dangerously low. Heads are heavy and mushy. Brain cells inert.

I hadn't bothered to plan this lesson. After all, they were really motoring on Dickinson now, so I thought this was going to be a no-brainer. All I had to do was give them a stimulating Starter and then they could get into groups and brainstorm around each section, and then feedback at the end. Teaching the teacher. The best kind of lesson.

We stared at images of the nervous system, a heart, feet, tombstones, watches, quartz, lead, a frozen landscape.

'Come on. Someone . . . Anyone,' I sighed.

The clock seems to have stopped.

'Ella?'

'Dunno.'

'Liam?'

'Er . . . sorry. What was the question?'

'Which. Poem. Is. This?'

'Cemetery?'

'What else?'

'Rolex.'

'OK. What else?'

'Stones. Heart. Feet.'

'Mmm-hmm. Anything else?'

'Winter.'

'Good. So what do we think the poem is about? Ella?'

'She's in love with this guy, yeah, but he dies, yeah, and den she goes to the cemetery in winter and den loses her watch. And den she gets bare cold and her feet get frozen and fall off?'

'Great, Ella! It's a start. OK. Couple of minutes to discuss it and then feedback.'

I checked my email. The Data Manager had sent round a reminder that the Year 7, 8 and 9 data was due, with a link to the spreadsheet and a SMART Notebook guide of how to fill in the columns.

The Year 11 Football Team had won another competition.

A reminder to get all reply slips in for the Oxford trip.

Tick, tick, tick. Delete all. Delete all the emails! LA LA LA!

They are still just sat there.

I turned the lights off.

(We need the dark. To dwell in shades of doubt and ambiguity.)

I told them to put their heads on the table, to empty their minds and just drift, as I read the poem as quietly as I could.

After great pain, a formal feeling comes –
The Nerves sit ceremonious, like Tombs –

I was aware of a figure at the door.

Tom! Good timing. I loved it when Tom came into lessons. We always had fun – we put on wigs and pretended to be poncey critics, which we enjoyed, even if the kids didn't.

'Hello, Sir!' I said. 'Great timing. Come in. Come in! We were just struggling with this poem. Come and help us out.'

Tom nodded once and asked if he could sit at the back.

'Sure. Sure, why not? You can help Ella.'

Tom sat down next to Ella as I carried on reading.

'"The Feet, mechanical, go round –" OK, what kind of imagery is that? Anyone? Hmm? Anyone? The feet mechanically going round. What does that make you think of? Isaac? . . . Zainab? . . . OK, everyone bang their feet on the ground. Now bang them mechanically. What do you notice? . . . Anyone? . . . Why don't you discuss it in your pairs for one minute and then feedback.'

While they discussed, I walked over to Tom and whispered, 'I think you freaked them out!' He didn't say anything.

After the minute was up, I picked on Wally, who guffed on about the juxtaposition of machinery and Christianity and the industrial revolution, and how feet point in different directions in different sexual positions. And how she was not getting enough. Alexia laughed, so Wally got angry and defensive and said, 'What?'

Silence returned.

'"A Quartz contentment, like a stone –" What about that image? Extraordinary, don't you think? "Quartz contentment". One minute to discuss.'

The odd murmur. Tom talked to Ella in a low voice. I heard the word 'prediction' before he asked to see her folder. She reluctantly pulled it out of her bag and showed it to him. He flicked through it, then took out his iPad and made some notes. He moved on, mechanical, from Isaac – who had forgotten his folder – to Wally – whose folder was covered in Tippex dicks – to Alexia – whose folder was bursting at the seams with everything ever written about Dickinson from the internet packed into plastic covers – to Zainab, whose folder was pristine, with every full-mark essay typed up and covered in lovely bulbous green pen.

He nodded once in my direction, and walked out.

At the end of the lesson, I put my email address on the board so they could send me their work. None came through. They all protested that they had sent it to me.

I searched through the database for myself.

And there I was. My name, but next to an empty icon. A dark silhouette with no distinguishing features. I clicked on it.

No face, no details, nothing.

A cypher.

A doppelgänger.

A ghost in the machine.

Why would they create a doppelgänger for me?

Maybe I am being disappeared.

Maybe I am already Invalid.

I went back to the Department and patted Tom on the back.

'Hey, thanks for coming in and livening up the morgue! God, they were so dead!'

He turned and looked at me with a dead-eyed shark stare. I asked if he was all right as I waved my hand in front of his face.

'Bueller? *Bueller?*'

He took his iPad out and opened the Observation App.

'What was going on in that lesson?' he asked, combatively.

'What do you mean?'

'Why did they have their heads on the desk?'

'I had to try something. You know what they're like at the end of the day. I wanted to let them drift and connect with the poetry.'

'Right. I see.'

He made some notes on his iPad. I asked him what he was writing, but he ignored me.

'Then there was all the banging on the floor,' he said.

'Right. Kinaesthetic. Aural. Yeah?'

'I've been looking at their mock results.'

'Oh?'

'They're not great.'

'No, but we hadn't read many poems when they took that. They know them much better now.'

'I'm concerned. We're all concerned.' He waved in the general direction of Death Star Command.

'Every time I come past, they don't seem to be writing.'

'No, we are discussing. And engaging.'

'Why didn't Ella know what her prediction was?'

'I don't know. Because she's a moron?'

He nodded a slow, deliberate nod.

'She's working at around a C, right?'

'A very generous C.'

'What bothers me is that she did not know what she needed to do to be getting a B.'

'What? You know Ella. But she's getting better all the time. She's more confident in class, coming up with loads of stuff.'

'She didn't seem to know much about the poetry.'

He pressed a cross on his screen.

'I could only find three pieces of marked work in their folders,' he continued. 'By my calculations, they should have eight essays, printed off and annotated in green pen with teacher–student dialogue.'

'We did essays in class at the beginning of term. But since then they have been doing presentations and coursework; researching; you know, independent learning? What we've been trying to get them to do? Weaning them off our drained, withered teats?'

'They need to do well in their coursework.'

He nodded another singular, deliberate nod.

'What are you suggesting?' I asked.

'By the end of the day you need to have your coursework marks adjusted so once added with their mocks they are in line with their predictions. You need to turn the spreadsheet green.'

'But that would be a lie.'

'Not if that's what they are going to get.'

Another singular nod.

'No. No, not if that is what they are going to get,' I said, as I nodded hypnotically in unison.

'I've marked you down as Inadequate in this Informal Observation,' said Tom, as he clicked a button on his iPad, turned and walked back down the hall, as if being recalled back to his charging station.

Tom was being disappeared before my eyes.

Nobody knows exactly how they do it. One minute, a teacher is there – present, affable, joyous – the next, they're gone. Not physically gone, just *gone*: vacant, impassive, unresponsive. Gone.

I couldn't really blame him. Or them. It's just the way it goes. It was time. He was ready to go to the next level. I knew he was being targeted. They had started button-holing him in the playground. I saw him at lunchtime, bending over, listening intently to their secret orders; when I walked past, they hushed up. I said, 'What was all that about?' He said, 'Oh, just about the PTA Fun Run.' But I knew it wasn't. Little Miss Outstanding was doing the PTA Fun Run. At least, that's what she told me.

He was taken over the long weekend. I don't know where they took him, exactly; some faraway place – a wood or glen or nuclear power station. Some say it is an expensive country hotel, which has a spa and complementary Spin lessons.

What they do there is a mystery. Apparently, there is a lot of talk of being 'aligned' with company values. I bet they 'align' them. Stretch them out. Waterboard. Play Beethoven's Ninth. Electrocute to images of books and flowers. Eat data. Go Spin.

The next thing I knew, he was the new Ho6 (the Zen floater had already been given the boot). And it was never the same again. Assemblies with Ho6 used to be the highlight of my week. They were like a cross between a picnic and a stand-up routine. She used to talk about herself as a kid, bunking off school; she showed pictures of the hill she used to sit on and read poetry. She teased the kids, saying it was the equivalent of her chicken-and-chip shop. She could tease them, because she had built their trust over the years, and they knew she had their backs and she loved them. That meant she could also teach them, so when her assembly segued into a rousing panegyric about love and beauty, they lapped it up. They wanted to read more because they wanted to be like her. I remember one assembly when she told them about her English teacher. She said he had changed her life. Then she broke down in tears.

Now the whole Sixth Form stared straight ahead as Tom put up photographs of the Common Room and berated students for leaving it in such a mess.

Weekly Form Meetings with Ho6 used to involve eating croissants underneath verses of *Paradise Lost*. We were of the Devil's Party. She was our Princess Leia, and this was where the Rebellion was forged.

Tom was an Imperial Guard now, so there was no levity any more. We just looked at print-offs of absences. He tried to give it a slight whiff of anarchy by introducing an

Attendance Challenge. Every week, whoever had the best attendance got a bag of mini-eggs. My attendance always hovered around the 95 per cent mark, mostly thanks to Wally, so I never got the mini-eggs. Little Miss Outstanding had 100 per cent attendance every week, but then she had all the keenies in her form. I was sure Tom was marking me down for this somewhere on that iPad of his.

He probably has a mini-egg App. There's Little Miss Outstanding's head over a full basket; that's my head over the empty one.

All SMs really cared about was what could be measured and tallied on a spreadsheet. Results. Attendance. Reply Slips. They knew we wouldn't give a shit about the Reply Slips. Suddenly, Tom was all about the Reply Slips.

Tom had asked for the Reply Slips from each form to prove that the parents had seen a letter telling them about the trip to Oxford. Only Little Miss Outstanding had her Reply Slips signed and returned and handed back in a plastic folder, clipped together with a paper clip. A couple of others had a few dribs and drabs. But he made an example of me.

'Where are they?'

I pulled out a wodge from my pocket.

'I've got a few.'

'Where are the rest?'

'They say they'll bring them in. But you know what they are like. This is Ella, Wally, Isaac.'

'Exactly why we need to follow up. Have they seen the letter?'

'I gave it to them. It passed beneath their eyes for at least a moment. What else can I do?'

'When I came past your form room most of the letters were in the recycling bin.'

'That was after I left –'

'Did you note down on the spreadsheet who had taken them?'

I hadn't. I was afraid of spreadsheets, as well he knew. It was the only part of teacher training that I failed. ICT proficiency. I had to tally on a spreadsheet all the students who were coming to Alton Towers on a school trip. It took me the allotted three minutes to fill in the column denoting how many needed vegetarian packed lunches, when the time ran out.

He handed me a fresh stack of letters, with his name digitally inscribed on the signature line.

'This is the time of year we have to be most vigilant,' he explained, as if talking to a Year 7 Set 4 who had not done his homework. 'This is when the Isaacs and the Wallys are starting to fall through the cracks. If we keep following up on the small stuff, the big stuff will follow. I need you to phone home and find out who knows about this.'

The next day I instigated a Reply Slip amnesty.

'OK, everyone. I really need you to give me that Reply Slip.'

'Which reply slip?'

'The Reply Slip that says that your parent or guardian has seen the letter.'

'Which letter?'

'The letter about the trip to Oxford.'

'What trip to Oxford?'

'The one that's next week! The one I've been telling you about for a month!'

'Sorry. Forgot, sir.'

'Lemme go Oxford!'

At lunchtime, I called all the parents. The conversations went the same way.

'Hello? Is that Liam's mum?'

'Yes?'

'Hi. It's Mr Teacher. Liam's Form Tutor.'

'Oh God, what's happened?'

'No, no, nothing. Nothing bad. Liam's fine.'

'Is he not working again?'

'No, it's not that. I mean, he's got a little better since our last conversation. He still has a way to go, but that's another conversation. No, the reason I am calling, Miss Donaghue, is about a trip to Oxford I am organising. Did Liam give you the letter?'

'No.'

'Ah. He should have.'

'OK. When is it?'

'It's next Tuesday.'

'OK. What time do I need to be there?'

'You don't. It's just for him.'

'OK. So . . .?'

'No, it's just I need you to sign the letter which says that you've seen the letter. And that you are happy for him to come. To Oxford.'

'Can't I just tell you? Now? Over the phone?'

'No. I really need the Reply Slip. Can you please just sign it? I'm so sorry.'

I ended up faking all the parents' signatures and handing the reply slips back to Tom. He didn't even say thank you.

That Friday, I had to do Homophobia in Meedja. At the beginning of the lesson, I asked if anyone was homophobic. They all said they weren't. After a discussion, we established they *all* were, even the ones who thought they weren't (all except the Muslim girl who said, 'My parents taught me to cherish all people'). I told her I wished we all had her parents, then got really angry with the others, put on *Queer as Folk*, and stormed out, telling them to write down diegetic and non-diegetic sounds on their table. Tom came in when I was out of the room. When I came back in, he nodded at me, and made a note on his iPad.

Then Year 11. Unseen Poetry. 'Hurricane Hits England' by Grace Nichols. We were having a pretty chilled lesson, just doing a bit of gentle analysis.

Rich was sat next to Janice. They made a funny pair because they were so limby – four long legs stretched out under the desks. Tom came in, nearly tripped, sat down at the back, took out his iPad.

'What is the meaning of trees falling as heavy as whales?' I asked.

Silence.

Finally, Janice said casually, to no one in particular, 'Imagine if a whale fell on you.'

Long silence. I wasn't sure if they were thinking about what she had said, or about the poem, or about something else entirely.

Tom raised his chin, leant forward and scanned the room for signs of life, like a lighthouse sweeping the ocean.

'I'd probably survive,' said Rich, scratching his crotch.

Long silence.

Tom made a note on his iPad and walked out, carefully stepping over their legs.

Then I had a cover lesson, in which the Biology teacher had forgotten to set cover, so they were farting around with the gas taps all lesson. During my well-earned Free, I ate a Cheese String and tried to replace all the hyphens in my Dickinson revision booklet. I was measuring a hyphen when an email arrived.

From: Head of Sixth Form
Subject: Library
Hey, I know how you are a big fan of the Library. Fancy going there later?

At last! My old mucker is back!

I emailed back that I would see him there at four. As I wrote, another email arrived.

From: Head of Sixth Form
Subject: Email Recalled.

And with that, all our correspondence disappeared.

I went to the Library at 4 p.m. as usual. Tom was there, at the bar, talking to another teacher. I went up to Tom and patted him on the shoulder and said, 'What gives?'

He looked nonplussed.

'You recalled your email!'

Still nothing.

'You sent me an email saying you would see me here. And then you recalled it.'

He shrugged and looked away.

'Sorry. Wrong teacher.'

He went to talk to another teacher. Probably the cipher who gets sent all the essays. The Other Teacher. His New Best Bud.

I left, heartbroken, into the night. As I walked past the estate, I saw Kieran surrounded by Puffa fish, laughing and jostling and wolf-whistling at Mercedes, who was walking on the other side of the road.

I ran the rest of the way home.

My Personal Best.

15

Go Oxford

Everyone wanted to go Oxford. Everyone.

They were emboldened by how many had got in last year (whose names were now displayed on a zinc board in the Canteen) and by the Outreach efforts of the university. Every month or so an Outreach officer from an Oxbridge college would come to give a presentation in Assembly, which depicted happy, diverse castles of light. Black, white and brown female students lounged on the quad grass, punted, fenced and threw their mortar boards into the air. Finally, after centuries of discouragement, the 93 per cent were in with a shot of making it to the hallowed groves of academe.

There were those, like Alexia, who stood an excellent chance; there were those, like Liam, who thought they had a chance, and needed to be told to give up before causing undue heartache for all concerned; and then there were those, like Ella, who didn't have a chance in hell, but wanted a day out in Hogwarts.

Organising the trip was a bureaucratic clusterfuck. I had to get the trip approved with SM; then I had to draft a letter for the kids to give their parents, which explicitly stated **in bold** how much money they needed for the bus, and that they had to bring in their **discount cards**, and that they would be back around **11 p.m.** so their parents could decide whether to tick the box that said they would **pick them up** or were **happy for them to come home alone**; then I had to print off all the personal data of the kids who were coming with all the contact details of the kids *and* their parents *and* all their medical information, which for some reason produced, like, *fifty* sheets of data, some of it replicated over and over; one girl apparently had **BOWEL PROBLEMS BOWEL PROBLEMS BOWEL PROBLEMS** – like that sounds **horrendous** – three times **in bold**, we just shouldn't let her on the coach; then I sent an email in the morning to Form Tutors with a big red exclamation mark reminding them to remind students to get work from those teachers whose lessons they were missing; then I had to field a lot of arsey emails from teachers who didn't realise I was taking a trip and how disruptive it was to their learning; then I had to chase around the building for those who had forgotten and drag them out into the playground.

They stood in a line in the playground as I took a paper register.

Everyone but Liam.

Fuck's sake. Fucking Liam.

I consulted my sheet and found Liam's number. I called his mum, who was apologetic, and said he was on his way, and that he was bringing his Reply Slip in with him. I said, 'Thanks, but you can just tell me over the phone: are you happy for him to come home alone?'

She said she was.

Really? Are you sure? The guy's a complete cretin.

Just as I was giving up on Liam, I heard the *swish swish* of the giant blue Puffa, and turned to see him running across the playground.

Tom and I designated group leaders, gave a final pep talk about how they were all ambassadors of the school and had to be on their best behaviour, *yadda yadda*, and we trooped off to the station.

Buying tickets for the bus was unfeasibly traumatic. Despite all the haranguing and letters adorned with bold imperatives, some of the kids still managed to screw it up. Either they did not have enough money, or they had forgotten their discount card, or they had forgotten everything. The bus was going to leave, so I screamed at them to get on the bus and promised that I would pay for any who did not have tickets.

We all crammed onto the top of the bus. Smart entrepreneurial types peered over their newspapers suspiciously. Who could blame them? In their giant Puffas, caps and trainers, my charges had reverted to common-or-garden hoodlums. In the space of a day, a reverse alchemy had taken place: the gold had been returned to base metal. I was pretty freaked out by them and I was their guardian.

The bus lurched off, sending Wally crashing over a woman who spilt her coffee on her blouse. I took a quick register. It felt good to assert control.

Don't worry, folks. I've got this.

We left town.

Into the dark unknown. I thought about my Year 8s, and their narrow *Weltanschauung*. We should have got a plane. Here be dragons. Here be exurbs: airfields, Carphone Warehouses, golf courses, Tescos. A chorus of 'go Tescos'.

The kids settled down and quietly revised or twiddled with their phones. Liam was reading *Marketing for Dummies*; Alexia hoovered up *Nights at the Circus*; Ella was reading a copy of the local newspaper she had found on the seat, which had an article about a recent gang murder. She was pointing at the boy in the photograph and saying that she knew him and babbling on about who was shanking who and so on.

As the green fields and open skies of Albion unfurled before us, the conversation changed. Everyone calmed down, and became lost in reverie. Liam asked if a cow was a cow. Wally teased Liam that a shed was his house. I shut my eyes and let the babbling lull me to sleep.

I was woken by Ella tapping me on the shoulder.

'Oi, Sir. Oi, Sir. Sir!'

'What is it, Ella?'

'Innit, Sir, dat's a peanut factory?'

After about a half an hour, Tom ushered me to the back of the bus conspiratorially. He checked that no one could hear him, then explained to me in a very loud whisper that things were not as they seemed. While we were all going to Oxford, not all of us were going to Oxford *University . . . If you get my drift . . .*

I didn't get his drift.

The likely candidates – *your Alexias, your Zainabs, your Wallys* – were going to go with him to a big fat Oxford college. The rest were going to come with me to Oxford Brookes. I asked if he had told them this. He blushed and said that he hadn't, not exactly, not in so many words.

'So we lied to them?'

'It's fine. It will seem as if you are going to a different college.'

'But when we get to the big sign that says OXFORD BROOKES . . .?'

'Walk quickly. You're good at that now.'

I had to get my lot off the bus before everyone else, so as we approached our stop I went around the bus saying, 'Come on! Let's get off here! No, not you. You!' Which was met with great confusion and protestation.

Ella, Isaac, Liam and the rest of the rabble stood on the pavement, demanding an explanation. I told them it was fine. We were just checking out another college. We'd see the rest later.

After an underwhelming tour, Liam whispered to me that 'This ain't Oxford.' I told him to suck it up. The dissent grew dramatically during the three-hour 'interactive session' in the lecture theatre in which student reps nervously explained student grants. At the end of the session, the student reps decided that it was a good idea for everyone to write down their feedback on a piece of paper and throw it at them as a paper airplane. As the airplanes bombed down upon the beleaguered reps heads I made an executive decision to cut our losses and get the fuck out.

We stood on top of the hill, admiring the honeyed rooftops of the place where we were not welcome. Liam asked why we couldn't go with the others. I said that while he definitely had the ability – which he did, on his day – a rare day, admittedly – one day a week, perhaps – a day remarkable in its, and his, shining perspicacity, unsullied by skunk and World of Warcraft – his predictions weren't good enough. He wasn't having any of it. I explained that it wasn't that we were saying he was too thick to go to Oxford. It was that we were *predicting* he would be too thick.

It was a nonsense. We had to go. I marched them down the hill and breached the medieval defences of the town.

Once in the centre of town, we looked up at the imposing heads of the Greek Philosophers bearing down at us while we established that they were not anyone's mum. I guided them into the Porter's Lodge of one of the more 'liberal' colleges, one of the ones which have something approaching a representative number of state-school kids, women and gay discos. Where some graduates aptually don't go into the Tory party.

'Wassa Porter?' asked Ella.

'Is it a toilet?' asked Liam.

'They keep a dragon in the back quad,' I said, as we passed through the front quad. 'So if you are a particularly gifted student, they might let you be dragon-keeper.'

We sat down in the dining hall with hundreds of other kids. A man in a gown stood on the stage and looked out nervously at the tapestry of blazers and Puffas. Behind him was a slide with photos of Benazir Bhutto and Aung Sang Suu Kyi, enlarged (Boris Johnson and David Cameron had been reduced in size, and pushed towards the margin of the slide). He finished his talk by declaring that the purpose of education was 'Light, Liberty and Learning'. I felt a great stirring in my soul.

Strolling back across the quad towards the Buttery, Ella started laughing and saying, 'Is this where all the butters students are?' I told her to be quiet, as she perched awkwardly on a giant oak chair and was handed a champagne flute full of orange juice.

'Only posh people drink juice from champagne glasses,' said Liam.

'Innit,' agreed Ella.

We met up with the others, who seemed to have had a lovely time. Wally was particularly energised; he grilled the students about which societies he should join – he was keen on Ultimate Frisbee – and had worked out exactly which room he was going to have (near the bar, so it was just a short stumble back, nudge nudge).

We ambled through the squares and cobbled streets in silence. Every statue, every gargoyle, looked down with disdain, stubbornly refusing to give up its secrets. Through the grand gates and onto Christchurch Meadow, crunching along the gravel of the broad avenue, lined with poplars, which leads to the river, watching rowers gently sculling over the water. We turned around and gazed over the fence at the Constable painting before us: fringing the horizon were russet and brown leafless trees, like arterial X-rays, and towers spiking audaciously into the sky; in the foreground, cows and bulls with giant horns huddled in the corner, munching on tufts of long grass coated with frost. There was silence, graceful silence, but for the low-ing of the cows and the pealing of a distant bell. The fog from our breath joined the stubborn layer of haze that sat a few feet above the grass, obscuring the cows, and making it seem as if the entire city was hovering on a cloud. I thought about my English teacher, who claimed to have had a duel on the meadow with a Polish count over a girl, which was why he had a scar on his cheek.

I never told him what he meant to me.

I should.

And Dad. And Granddad. This was their view.

Oxford begat Oxford begat Oxford. The secret rule of the game.

A profound melancholy gripped me and I shuddered, pulling my scarf up over my mouth.

'Y'a'right, Sir?'

'Fine thanks, Ella. You see those cows? Those are Clinton's cows. You know why they are called that? Because Bill Clinton donated them to the university.'

'No wonder dey're so horny.'

We saw an old lady sitting on a bench, with a large bag beside her, sketching leaves. She looked up at us briefly, then returned to her sketch. We stood beneath Christchurch and looked up at the looming patriarchal edifice.

'It looks burnt.'

'True say. Burnt and sad.'

'It's like Hogwarts.'

'Or Jordan.'

'Is dat where you sleep?'

'Yup.'

'Naaaah!'

'You can't sleep in there! Bet there's bare ghosts.'

I told them that the teachers slept there too; and they had to go to tutorials in their bedrooms.

'Urghh!' shouted Liam. 'Dat's NASTY. Why?'

'That's the way it works. Twice a week you stay up all night, hastily scribbling a wretched essay which you can't remember anything about, go into some old duffer's bedroom, read the essay, and then leave. The teaching is shocking. I spend more time on my Year 8s than these Dons do on their precious undergrads. Too wrapped up in their weird worlds. Lacking even the basic communication skills. You can leave this place without having learned a thing. But it will stand you in good stead, because once you are armed with the special skill of hastily cobbling together some bollocks you know nothing about, you can confidently go out and run the country.'

'Hmm. Maybe it's not for me after all,' said Liam.

We walked back through the gathering gloom, out of which emerged pasty faces, ravaged by acne, with black eye sockets of unfathomable angst. Long lines were form-ing outside a pair of kebab vans, squatting and thrum-ming in the dusk.

'Rah, they got everything here.'

'Chips, Cheese *and* Beans?'

'No way.'

'NO. WAY.'

'What did I tell you, kids? Welcome to Arcadia.'

After we had bought a selection of disgusting polystyrene-based snacks, we walked towards the bus stop. Suddenly, I grabbed Liam by the shoulder and pointed upwards. There, above a giant portico, was a tri-angular dark-blue crest, with three gold crowns around a gold-leafed book, emblazoned with the words 'DOMINUS ILLUMINATIO MEA'.

'No way! No way!'

Liam grabbed Ella and showed her. Then she grabbed Isaac. Soon they were all looking up shouting, 'Oooooh!!!!! 'LUMINATI!!!'

At the Martyr's Memorial, Alexia recited, 'We shall this day light such a candle, by God's grace, in England, as I trust shall never be put out.'

'Wassat?' said Liam.

'Latimer to Ridley as they were burnt alive for heresy. It's in *Fahrenheit 451*.'

'Yeah. Yeah, I knew dat.'

On the bus, I felt a wave of relief. All we had to do was get on the bus and then a short walk back to school. What could go wrong?

The bus rattled through the darkness. Liam and Ella cuddled up on the back row, while the others propped their heads against the windows and looked forlornly at their reflections.

After about fifteen minutes, the bus pulled into a dark, forbidding place. A solitary figure stood alone. As our glancing eyes passed him, his face was briefly illuminated by the carriage lights. It was a terrifying sight: a spectral, gaunt visage pointed upwards towards Brylcreemed hair, on top of which was perched a small military hat. He wore a long trenchcoat and over one shoulder was slung a large bag, which was about the size of a Kalashnikov.

The other thing I didn't foresee in my trip application.

He stepped onto the bus, turned and stared at us. Ella whimpered, hid behind the seat and whispered, 'Sir, what shall we do?'

'I don't know, Ella. Why don't you call one of your friends?'

'Which ones?'

'The ones in the gang.'

'Dey wouldn't be seen dead out here! Come on! You've got to do something!'

She's right. What to do? Where the hell was this in teacher training? My noble chivalry is at stake. I should challenge him to a duel.

'Sir. Sir! Shall we rush him?' whispered Liam.

'No, don't be ridiculous.'

The man stepped a couple of steps closer and thrust his crotch forward, so it was inches away from Isaac's nose, then slowly inserted his thumbs under his belt. Liam whimpered and clutched onto Ella. I took control and beckoned them into a huddle.

'OK, everyone. When I say run ... we run for the door,' I whispered.

Whimpers of assent.

The man took another step closer.

'RUN!'

Just as the bus was about to leave, I ran to the emergency button, and pressed it, shouting. ''Scuse me, we forgot – this is our stop!'

The doors opened. I grabbed Puffa after Puffa and hurled them screaming into the cold night.

We huffed and puffed and held our sides as the bus pulled away. I gathered everyone together, calmed them down, did a quick head count. Liam was bent over with laughter.

'Oh, my daze! What were you playing at? He was just going to some kinky club up in town!'

'Freak.'

'What do we do now?'

I looked around. The wind was picking up and biting. Thunder rumbled across the hills.

'Just stay close. And stay warm.'

Liam cuddled Ella under his jacket. Zainab asked if there was any room for her too.

'Sir, I don't reckon I want to go Oxford after all,' said Liam.

'It's their loss, Liam. What are you going to do instead?'

'Dunno yet, Sir. Maybe I'll take a year off and think about it.'

'What would you do on your gap year?'

'Dunno. Maybe try to get to Level 15. Do a Dungeon Run.'

'Well, you've got to have goals.'

'Anyone else want to go Oxford?' I asked. 'Zainab?'

Zainab wrinkled her nose.

'No, please! Don't do this to me! You have to! It would be criminal not too!' I pleaded. 'What about you, Alexia? You're in, surely?'

Alexia shrugged.

'Anyone else?'

'Reckon I might stay at home,' said Isaac.

'Don't have to pay rent. Avoid weirdos,' said Ella.

'And cows,' said Isaac.

'Stay warm,' said Alexia.

'I'm all over it,' said Wally.

16

Isaac

He liked to draw the poems. He wasn't confident in writing or speaking in class, but was 'Gifted and Talented' nonetheless, particularly at art, so every lesson I let him draw the poem. On the walls of the classroom, between W. B. Yeats and Miles Davis, were sketches of gothic chambers and moonlit carriage rides.

He had 'stuff going on at home', as we say in the business. He was connecting to something darker within the literature. When I asked him for his initial response to a poem, he talked very fast – intensely, lucidly, imaginatively – and then tapered off, only to stare at the page in silence. It was like a flash of lightning illuminating deep darkness.

Orally, his ideas were extraordinary. But when he tried to put them down, there was a short circuit. As was often the case with creative students, the ideas were vivid and imaginative, but very weak in terms of structure and coherence, like this:

first – chill – then stupor then the letting go this shows that Emily is feeling cold which shows that maybe she has loss as if she is in morning the use of hyphens looks like sticks beating her down this shows that she is falling

When I gave his essays back he became very discouraged. I had used green pen (more encouraging than red) and lots of praise, but he didn't read my comments; he simply saw the mark, gasped, and slammed the essay on the table in disgust, shutting down for the rest of the lesson. I tried to encourage him, by printing off his and Alexia's essay for Peer Assessment, but it backfired. Rather than feeling that his ideas were equivalent to hers, and that he just needed to learn to refine his expression a little, he saw only a glaring gulf between them, and thought we were all patronising him. I persevered, reading out his essay. It was like reading beat poetry. We all agreed that he should write poems. For a sweet few weeks, he wrote poems in response to Emily's. And they were devastating.

But then the walls began to close once more. The pressure was ramping up, and he reacted very badly. The more he was pressured, the more he shut down. He stopped working across the board. Complaints rained in from all his teachers that he was falling dangerously behind. Even in Art.

His attendance became a Cause for Concern. If he did 'deign to grace us with his presence' – a phrase I had stopped using since he looked at me with a brow of thunder when I uttered it – I asked why he was late, but he did not reply as he plonked down behind the screen, still muffled by his coat. He had stopped asking anyone in form for work, too embarrassed to admit how far behind he was. His eyes became hooded and glacial. It looked like he had begun a heavy course of antidepressants. I tried to engage him, but he waved away my concern with brittle nonchalance, and stared into the screen like a man staring into a deep dark well.

I was worried that Emily, who had once energised him so, was now responsible for his melancholy. I lay awake worrying about him, thinking about him sitting there reading 'This World is not Conclusion', and rather than seeing it as a poem that should encourage us – that evolution and faith can be contradictory, that there are limits to our reason and that it is OK to be confused and full of doubts – he would see it only as confirmation that it was pointless to try and do anything.

'What's the problem now?' asked Amy at midnight.

'I think teaching English is a bad thing.'

'Why? I thought you were saving their souls. Leading them through "the vale of soul-making".'

'I think that might be a bad place for them to go. I think maybe they would be better off if they just didn't go there.'

He stopped handing in essays at all. At the end of the lesson, the other students handed in their essays while Isaac bolted for the door. The punishment for missing an essay was detention; for missing two, Parental Meeting. For missing three, we would have to refer him to Tom, put him on report, and review whether he should carry on with the subject. He had missed four, but I had yet to go through the proper channels. I was trying to protect him. I knew that if I told him he was in detention, he would overreact and not come to the next lesson. And fall further behind. And so it snowballs.

We set up non-punitive, non-judgemental 'meetings' after lessons, during break, lunch and after school, going through his last essay. I read it out loud, gushing over how wonderful the ideas were, and showing him how all he needed to do was just sort out the syntax and grammar. But even with all the red and green lines on his Word document, he couldn't see where he was missing capital letters, hyphens or even full stops. After our first couple of sessions, he seemed to be happy about how much he had improved his essays – from 5 out of 15 to 8 out of 15, for instance, but after the third essay, he started to feel discouraged. Like I was picking on him. After five minutes of our session, he turned and said, 'I don't know! I don't know what's wrong with it!'

'There's nothing wrong, Isaac,' I said. 'It's not wrong. Quite the opposite. It's brilliant. One of the best ideas I've heard. It just needs clarifying.'

'You always say that!' he screamed, with a ferocity that made me step onto the computer wires and disconnect his monitor. 'Why are you wasting your time?'

'I don't understand. What do you mean, Isaac?'

'Every lesson it's the same. You ask a question. Zainab or Wally or Alexia answer in perfect sentences. Everything they say sounds perfect. It sounds academic. It sounds like the right answer. They are *experts*. You are an *expert*. Why are you wasting your time with a fool like me?'

He walked out and didn't come back for two weeks.

We had a Parental Meeting, but it was impossible to get through to Mum. I got the impression that Isaac was looking after her, rather than the other way round.

March was the cruellest month. The coursework deadline was approaching. Teaching took a bath. It seemed like every kid in the school was in a computer room doing coursework.

As the final deadline approached, I said he had to give it to me after school that day, or he would have to redo the year. His hooded, glacial eyes stared straight through me. 'Good,' he said.

'Is that what you want? Is that what you really want?' I spluttered.

'Yes.'

'Look, Isaac,' I pleaded, as I shut the door of the Business Suite, and motioned for him to sit at a computer, 'I can't let that happen. I will never forgive myself. You will never forgive yourself. We're not leaving here until you put something – anything – on that page.'

We sat there for hours. Past detentions, past band practice, past play rehearsals, past the janitor emptying the bins. Six o'clock rolled around and he had written a paragraph with no full stops. Suddenly, he got up and said, 'I'm going. That's it. I need to go home and do it. I can't concentrate. I promise I will email it to you tonight.' I said I didn't believe him, and that if I did not have it by the morning, I would have to take him off the course. He waved me away as he rushed out into the night, forgetting his art folder in the Business Suite.

The next morning, I checked my inbox. He had sent it at 4.48 a.m. I printed it off and added it to the pile. When he arrived in form, looking desolate, I congratulated him and told him to chill out. Now we could just read, recite and write poetry for the rest of term. The walls had fallen away.

That weekend, I had to do all the marking in the world. Friday night, I was too tired. Saturday, I stared at the wall. On Sunday I procrastinated and procrastinated. Then I went for a run.

1.9 km – Split: 8.7 miles per hour.

By Sunday night, the kitchen table was covered higgledy-piggledy with coursework and mark schemes. Amy had to eat her dinner on her lap on the sofa. At eleven, she came in and saw me with my head in my hands. She asked if I was all right. I said I wasn't, that the coursework was all turd, that the students were all going to fail and that I was going to be fired. She took the card off the fridge and gave it to me.

'You're not going to be fired. You're the Best Teache in the World Ever,' she said as she sat on my lap and kissed me.

After she went to bed, I read through them again. Perhaps they weren't so bad. No, in fact, they were good. Great. Alexia's was the best – elegant, incisive and original. Zainab's was also full marks: a little more workman-like, but it was clear and answered the question (not to mention formatted perfectly). Wally's was rushed but lively. Ella missed the point completely, but fair play for getting it done at all.

At 2 a.m., I stared at Isaac's coursework.

Montag has escaped the alienation of the mechanical society he left behind. Perhaps he will help establish a better one by remembering the words in the book he will commit to memory. This suggests that by staying connected to books, which are a reflection of other people's thinking, we stay connected as human beings one to the other. Books, then, are an antidote to alienation.

That's really good.

Suspiciously good.

I Googled the most suspicious sentence. Sure enough, there it was. The whole shitshow. Thank you, enotes High School Teacher. You have just been complicit in Isaac's downfall.

We were reaping the whirlwind. We went to such lengths to help our students – differentiation, 'scaffolding' (essay plans, quote sheets) – that when they reached Sixth Form, they did not trust their own minds. It was like watching a great mist descend over the generations, like the mist of forgetting in *The Buried Giant*, whereby they gradually lost their memories, originality and spark. If I showed them where to look – which meant I had to take them to the computer room and tell them what to Google – and then gave them an essay plan, they would work hard and produce something decent, but workmanlike. I was helping them to get the marks, but I was taking away their originality. The critics they found on the internet became a critical crutch. I tried to show them that it was just a game, that 'a critic's job is to say a rhinoceros is not an elephant', but they did not trust their own voices. They were only seventeen, after all. Who really knows what they think then?

I could see Isaac doing it. Sitting in his room, staring at the empty white annotationless borders of the book, cursing himself for not writing anything down, wondering about whether to message Zainab, who was currently looking at her edition, with all its pink annotations and underlinings, and writing them up into another full-mark essay in her bulbous turquoise pen. A perfect script, for Sir to photocopy. Sir wouldn't even need to read it, just put it down on the photocopier and hand it out with that smug look on his face.

Here's how it is done.

So much better than yours.

You useless slug.

He clicked, opened Pandora's Box and descended into the vortex. Down and down he fell, through leagues of vacuity, hitting uncertain worlds, looking around for anything to moor himself, desperately trying to grasp onto a rung on the ladder of wobbly blue links.

I can't believe he has fallen for this. After all I had ranted about the fucking internet. Sure, it had finally broke down the walls. Now they had access to the riches of learning, which was previously the preserve of the elite. But they didn't know where to look. I showed them Wikipedia, the *London Review of Books*, the *New Yorker*, academic articles. They would skim, shrug, then click onto the next link. And the next. And the next. They seemed completely desensitised to all of it.

Lesson #433
The Medium Is the Mess of the Age.

Every lesson, I banged on and on about how going
on the internet was like shaking the epistemological
kaleidoscope while trying to make sense of the discon-
nected fragments; how it represents the end of attention,
and attention is culture, as William James said; how going
from a literate culture to a digital culture represents the
same shift as when writing replaced the oral tradition,
which made Plato fear that memory would be replaced
(I made them take old-fashioned notes, which caused all
manner of consternation); how being permanently connected only makes you anxious and unhappy; how the
whole thing was a desperate shouty competition, the
exact opposite of the quiet reflection needed for poetry;
how it was the end of critical authority – it was once possible, way back when I was a kid ('Was dat Roman times?'
asked Liam) to have a few great books on a shelf and refer
to them again and again, and that was your world, your
solace; but now culture was a deracinated free-for all, the
centre cannot hold; now we are in a relativistic universe,
English Literature is on the same plane as Meedja, it is
basically YouTube Studies with a sprinkling of poetry,
poetry that is difficult to read beneath the flashing ads;
there is no way of distinguishing between the opinions of
Harold Bloom, Germaine Greer and Billy McGinty in his
bedroom, it is all fair game after all, and all on the same
plane: an open forum, a great wall-less palace of light,
without definition or form or craft or care; just slap any

old shit up there and just click on anything, anything will do. In Jonathan Franzen's words, which you can Google, cut and paste: 'All the real things, the authentic things, the honest things are dying off.'

The kids were right to take the piss out of me. I had become an old fart.

I gave back their coursework.

I let everyone go, then kept Isaac back, as I pulled up an essay on my computer.

'What's this?' he said.

'You tell me.'

'Tell you what?'

'Why have I got that essay on my screen?'

'Dunno, Sir.'

'You've never seen that before?'

'What is it?'

'Who wrote that?'

'Dunno, Sir.'

'You sure about that?'

'Yes, Sir.'

'*You* said that, Isaac.'

He paused and gaped a little.

'Did I?'

'Yes. What did you mean by that?'

'Erm –'

'The plagiarism is so obvious it is embarrassing. It doesn't read anything like you. I wish it did, because you can write. If you had written everything you had just said in class, you would have an A. Plagiarism is a very serious crime. Next time, at least change the font.'

I told him I had spoken to Head. The punishment was a week's suspension. He started weeping and giant snot bubbles blew out of his nose, like a whale's spume.

I was worried what he might do, so I filled in a Cause for Concern form and sent it to Tom. He didn't acknowledge it. I just carried on teaching, with Isaac sometimes present and sometimes not. I challenged Tom in the hallway. Tom said that we were in an impossible bind; Isaac refused to work, but was old enough that he had to check himself into Social Services. As he refused to do that, we had to just hope we could help him see the light. I saw a glimmer of compassion cross Tom's face. A pulse of life. The red Terminator light fading.

Isaac came back eventually, but we had to take him off the course. I tried to make him see that it was all going to be fine. That he could still go to Art College. He didn't need English. Reading is for life.

He didn't say anything. He had been conditioned to think that university was the only barometer of success. I told him his Art was far more important. But he couldn't see that. In the eyes of the school and society, he had failed, and there was nothing I could say to convince him. Everywhere he looked, he saw a system that valued what he struggled with.

I had failed him, because I had overwhelmed him with other voices, before I had let him truly trust his own.

Lesson #468
You've Just Got To Say What You Feel,
Not What You Ought To Say.

17

Triangulation for the Nation

ALL STAFF: URGENT
There will be an URGENT briefing in the
auditorium this afternoon at 4.30 p.m.

There were grave faces all round. The Doom-mongers of the Department thought that a student must have committed suicide. We tea-tottered up to the auditorium in silence.

Head addressed us as if he was announcing that we were going to war.

'I want to thank you all for staying behind after school. The news that we have been expecting has arrived.'

Humanities grabbed hold of each other, whimpering.

'The day that many of us had feared is now upon us.'

The French teacher exhaled like a horse.

'We are to be Ofstedded.'

Music laughed. Maths cheered. Humanities wept.

'OFSTED have informed us that they will visit some time over the next week. But do not worry. It is not something to fear. It is something to embrace. So after this briefing, I want everyone to go back to their departments and prepare for battle.'

Back in the Department, we leant on desks nervously, looking at HoD for guidance.

'What?' he shouted, defensively. 'What do you want me to say? We're an Outstanding department. You are all Outstanding teachers. Just do what you do. Come on! Seriously. What's got into you? I go into your lessons regularly and most of the lessons I see are Good or Outstanding. Don't change a thing.'

'But how do you know that what *they* are looking for is the same thing that *you* look for?' chipped in Mentor.

'Look, I know these people. I've worked with the fuckers. They're all failed teachers. They will always be looking for the thing you're not doing. That's their modus operandi. So just do what you do best. As long as your books are marked to buggery, we put up some nice displays of kids' work, and you don't get so freaked out you can't speak, we're going to be fine.'

Of course we would be fine. We were great. Weren't we? And we could just do what those other schools do and put all the naughty kids in the Portakabin round the back of the bike sheds.

And so the Terror returned.

Everything ramped up to warp factor gazillion. We were all to be on our guard at all times. Total vigilance. Never relax, never settle. You never know when they might appear and just OFSTED you.

We got the green pens out every lesson. Teaching took another bath. No chance of learning any new poetry, or performing the next scene. We just went back over all the old essays and covered them in green pen.

Book Peeks were over; entire sets of books were now piled up in Departments for Book Examinations. The sharks were at the door every lesson. But they didn't just hover. They were diving into the tank, devouring, ripping, crunching bones. Clouds of blood drifted up the glass. The wounded and dying hobbling around with stumps where their legs or arms once were. It was a massacre. Everyone Inadequate.

At the point of barest stress, another email.

```
URGENT!!!
REMINDER: Twilight Session today!!!
```

I clicked on the digital envelope. The envelope opened; an invitation floated upwards; the invitation unfolded to reveal a page of ornate calligraphy:

You are cordially invited to a CPD Twilight Session: 'Mastery and Proficiency in Classroom Observation. Part 1: MOPCEF – The Basics' Auditorium, 4.30 p.m. Please bring your iPads. Charged.

It was time for a session with the Educational Leadership and Development Consultant. Little Miss Outstanding could barely contain herself.

The rumour was that he had become a Consultant after he had turned around a failing school.

'I thought we had already been turned around?' I said.

233

'He wants to turn us back round the other way again,' said HoD.

We researched him on the internet. There was a fawning interview in a soft-focus digizine and lots of tweets, most of which seemed to consist of gnomic aphorisms plucked from Brainyquote, like 'Education is the art of making man ethical' and 'Achievement is the horse; self-esteem is the cart.' All we really needed to know was that he was one of *them*. A *Future Leader*. Like Blake in *Glengarry Glen Ross*, he had come from downtown on a mission of mercy to transform us deadbeats into high-performing, high-octane Cityslickers.

He had been into a few lessons already. Mentor had volunteered. She was always Outstanding, after all. He went to see her Year 9 Set 4s doing Roald Dahl's *Lamb to the Slaughter*, which seemed apt. Whereas most observers sit at the back for most of the lesson, Educational Consultant was busy, getting among the students' books from the get-go, obsessed with how much progress the student had made in the last week, half-hour, minute. After the lesson, she had gone to see him for what he called a 'Meta-Feedback Loop'. He ushered her onto a beanbag, while he ran his long fingernails around his mug of peppermint tea, saying, 'Make yourself comfy, make yourself comfy.' He said how much he enjoyed the lesson, then gave fair and constructive feedback.

He gave her a Good. Said she needed to show more 'Progress Over Time'.

She was spitting blood. 'How dare he! How dare he! Who the hell does he think he is! Coming in here with no knowledge of the kids or what we've been doing! I'll show him Progress Over Time!' she railed.

Four thirty rolled around. We were marking. No one moved. Suddenly, HoD got up and pushed a mug aggressively against the hot-water button. 'Oscar Wilde had it right. The problem with socialism is that there are too many meetings in the evening.'

'We have to bring our iPads. Charged.'

'I've lost mine.'

'I don't know my log-in.'

'Fuck. What is this wank? I've still got ten Year 9 books to mark.'

'It's all about the OFSTED. Just when you thought you could teach, along comes another tosser to tell you you were deluded.'

On the screen was a tree in a field, with someone sitting underneath it, reading a book. Underneath, in large, bold Calibri:

Someone's sitting in the shade today because someone planted a tree a long time ago.
– Warren Buffett

Educational Consultant greeted us as we entered the auditorium. He didn't just greet us – he *modelled* greeting us, his grin unwavering.

'Hello, Sir. *Hello, Sir.* Do help yourself to tea. Or coffee. Yes. Brownies. Don't hold back. And do please once you have your tea – or indeed coffee – please do sit back down and do get on with the "Starter" activity in your packs. Remember: this is a "Mixed-Ability Group", so we all work at different paces –'

On the first page:

> Quality is never an accident; it is always the result of high intention, sincere effort, intelligent direction and skilful execution; it represents the wise choice of many alternatives.
> – William A. Foster

HoD hitched up his trousers over his gut and muttered, 'Daddy, what does regret mean?' Little Miss Outstanding immediately started scribbling notes, while Mentor flicked through the pack.

'So many quotation marks.'

'And that's not counting the ones he is making with his fingers,' I said. 'Like every other word he's doing *that*.'

Educational Consultant clicked the clicker he had concealed in the arm of his suit jacket. The slide clicked onto the next slide, which read:

> Preamble #3
> Dispelling Some Myths
> (and one 'Ground Rule')

'Before we begin properly – and I realise I am asking a lot of you with so many "Preambles", but it is important as a "Mixed-Ability Group" that we dispel all preconceptions and prejudices before we begin. Today is not about judgement. I repeat: today is *not* about judgement. Always remember: you are not judging the performance of a teacher. Stop trying to! You are evaluating the impact of their classroom practice on the learning, progress and outcomes of the students. In doing so, your role is to then offer SMART action steps that will enable them to improve rapidly, continually and sustainably. Those are the Three Musketeers I carry around in my head: "Rapidity". "Continuity". "Sustainability". Now I am going to give you two minutes to talk through with the other professionals on your table the myths that you associate with classroom observation practice to date.'

We stared at one another.

'Is he speaking in tongues?' asked Mentor.

Educational Consultant clicked onto:

Ground Rule #1
Supportive Empowerment

'Some of us (I won't ask for names, we are a mixed-ability group here and as a believer in "AFL", I will be pulling lollypop sticks out of a cup if I want to enter the "Meta-Feedback Loop"), but some of us might be doing this for the first time. Let's embody our value of "Unity" to ensure we are supporting one another as we undertake the tasks throughout the session. Now I am very aware that time's chariot is charging towards us, so could I please ask you all to address The "Starter" activity that is on the second sheet of your "Twilight Session 1 Packs".'

4.47 p.m. We turned the page.

He clicked the clicker. There, in 72-point Calibri, with each letter a different colour:

MOPCEF

Suddenly the letters started moving, swimming around the board and reconfiguring into different variations.

PECFOM
POFECM
EOMFCP
FECMOP

'One minute to write down what you think "MOPFEC" stands for,' commanded Educational Consultant.

We wrote.

'OK, and in the spirit of "AFL", I am going to pull a lolly-pop out of the cup . . . and *voilà*: can I have Brian, please?'

Brian was in Maths. Brian must know.

Brian said, 'Monitoring Operations Practice Friendly Environmental Classroom?'

Educational Consultant winced.

'Nearly: Monitoring yes; Practice, yes; Classroom, yes . . .'

'Massive Orgasm Please For Every Class,' whispered HoD.

Educational Consultant picked another lollypop as fast as he could.

'Stuart? Where's Stuart? What do you think, Stuart? Go for it, Stuart.'

Stuart was in Science. Stuart must know.

'Monitoring Observational Practice of Classroom Evaluation Facility?'

Educational Consultant beamed.

'You're so close. *So* close. Really. I'll still give you a gold star! It is, in fact, "Monitoring Observational Practice of Classroom, Evaluation, Feedback".'

'Oh damn! So close!'

Educational Consultant moved to the next slide, a flow chart of Byzantine confusion:

Mastery and Proficiency in Classroom Observation:
'A Cyclical Methodology'

Arrows flowed around in a circulatory fashion, pointing at boxes crammed full of numbered, bold, italicised, bullet-pointed text:

Classroom Observation
Typicality
Teaching and Progress Over Time
Action Steps
SMART Targets
Observation Process
Evaluation
Judgements
Text-grade Match
Triangulation

'What the hell is triangulating?' I asked HoD.

'It's like circulating for socially awkward people like him.' Educational Consultant looked over.

'Is there some terminology you need clarifying?'

'Yes, please. I was struggling with "triangulation",' I said.

'Ah, yes. I am so glad you brought that up. In fact, I will currently make a note of it, so that I can add it to the list of terminology that needs clarification in the opening Learning Objective sequence of this presentation.'

'OK. Good. So what is it?'

Educational Consultant made two sides of a triangle shape with his arms. These quickly segued into quotation marks and then back to two sides of a triangle again.

'Ooooh! 'Luminati!' I said, impulsively, then realised I had said it very loud. Educational Consultant was looking at me like I usually looked at Liam.

'"Triangulation" is the process of observation whereby the observer examines the teacher's "Markbook", examines the targeted student's "Evidence", and finally engages in "Learning Discussion" with the targeted student.'

'So, sorry, what you're saying is: you look at the kids' books, write their marks down, and then talk to them about how they can improve?' said HoD.

'In layman's terms, yes, that is the beginning of triangulation, but by no means the end . . . Sir, if I may . . .' His arms were now in horizontal prayer. 'In order to make the requisite improvements to our profession, we must professionalise our language. Now for the "Observation Trail".'

'How disgusting,' said Mentor, retching on her shortbread.

'In this foci –'

We all started laughing. He was getting pissed off with English now.

'I really have to stop you there,' said Mentor indignantly. 'It is not "a foci". If it is singular, it must be "a focus".'

He didn't blink, and forged onwards.

'Now what I want to do is to try to replicate Stages 1 to 5 of the "Cyclical Methodology" process that we explored on the previous slide.'

He clicked on. Mercedes appeared on the board, beaming her big smile. Next to her was an enormous pie chart, and down the side were reams of data.

'So what I want you to do is log into your iPad and to enter the name of the student in the "Magnifying Glass" component of your Observation Trail database. Now you can see on the "Drop Down" menu all of the relevant data relating to the pupils in your class. In this case, we can see that Mercedes's "Gender" is "Female", her "Ethnicity" is "Black British", her "EAL Status" is "N", her "SEN Status" is "N", and we can see that she is on "Pupil Premium".'

Ah, dear Mercedes. How she loved the limelight.

He leapt down off the stage and stood next to a table with a single exercise book on it.

'So now it is time for the "Sage on the Stage" to give way to the "Guide on the Side".'

He held the green exercise book aloft.

I recognise that book.

Mercedes's book.

My book.

Shit, that's her English book.

Her book that I haven't marked, like, *all term*.

'Here we have Mercedes's English book. And if we look here –'

He flicked back through the book. Page after page of virginal work, unblemished by red or green pen.

'– we can see that this book has not been marked for some time. In fact, it does not seem to have been marked since . . . *January*.'

A collective gasp was unleashed, as if the entire auditorium had a puncture. Educational Consultant was piqued with pleasure. He was going to get one over on one of those arrogant English teachers, and he was going to do it by modelling patronising magnanimity.

'Let us approach these books in the spirit of "Non-Judgemental Development". And let us offer "Action Steps" for how the teacher could progress. Remember, an "Action Step" is not a "Target".'

After a torturous minute of 'Sage Time', he brought us back to the 'Meta-Feedback Loop' with a click of his widget. A cartoon Greek philosopher appeared on the screen with a giant speech bubble coming out of his beard that read, 'Feedback is the gift that keeps on giving.'

'So now what I would like you to do is "Microscript" your feedback response. Anyone?'

'He needs to mark his fucking books,' shouted HoD.

Nervous chuckles rippled across the room.

'Can we put that into more a more constructive "Meta-Feedback Loop"?'

'Sure.'

HoD turned to me.

'Mark your fucking books, douchebag.'

The next day, after a lesson in which Trainee pretended to be Rambo in order to teach antonyms (he had started bluescreening himself onto action films in order to teach things that had nothing to do with the topic in question, like becoming the Godfather for a lesson on the use of the modals), I met up with Mentor. I said I was sorry about the debacle with Mercedes's book – it was a rogue book, it had to be the one, all the others were up to date, I'd been focused on my 12s, *yadda yadda*. She was very understanding.

'Don't worry about the 8s. Your focus from now on has to be your Year 11s.'

She opened up an enormous spreadsheet. Mile upon mile of columns and rows, glowing red, yellow or green, with abbreviated headings. Pred. Mock. CW. S&L (deleted). Jan Entry (deleted). CW+Mock. Jun Lang. Jun Lit. Jun Lang+CW. UMS.

Data clusterfuck was in full effect.

Mentor had spent every spare moment painstakingly inputting every child's data, staying at school to 9 p.m. most evenings. She was now spending every spare moment explaining this terrifying Minotaur to her colleagues.

'Essentially, this is what they got last year. And this is their prediction for what they should get. And this is that converted into the new grading system. And this is their mocks. And this is their coursework. And this is their mock plus their coursework. And this is their mock plus their coursework converted into UMS. And this is the UMS converted into the new grading system. So here you can see your class and what they need to get in June to hit their predictions. Clear?'

I looked at my class list. Most flashed red. That meant that their mocks did not tally with their progress grades, which did not tally with the prediction I had given, which was based on the results of their last test, which I had massaged from the fake data given by the last teacher, who had given me this hospital pass by doing fuck all with them.

'This is crazy,' I said.

'I know. But we have to play the game.'

'You must spend all your time doing this.'

'Tell me about it. I trained to be a teacher, and I spend my whole time playing Battleships. But what choice do we have? The Powers That Be keep moving the goalposts, and we have to keep playing. What can we do? We can't call a Time Out. This is the most important year of these kids' education. And this is the most important subject. So. No pressure.'

Lesson #481

The Goalposts Keep Moving. Education
Wallahs Don't Trust Us or Our Results.
Every New Minister Has to Put Their Stamp
on Education and Reform for the Sake of It
by Insisting Things Change and Standards
Improve, Even If They Already Have,
Exponentially.

We went through my students and decided what kind of strategies I would need to employ to get them up to scratch, which meant doing practice papers with them until they bled. I was to target those on the C/D Borderline, because they were the ones who mattered the most: all that mattered was how many students we could cram into the A*–C league table.

Just as I was about to leave, she reminded me that we had a standardisation meeting with the Man from the Exam Board.

'Shit! Is that OFSTED?' I asked, quivering.

'No! Someone else big and scary.'

'Oh.'

'Do OFSTED want the same thing as the Exam Board?'

'Not really.'

'Oh.'

'It will all become much clearer. Maybe.'

It did not get clearer. It got much, much more opaque.

Marking English is a subjective business. That's the beauty of it. If I set you these questions, for instance:

Who is this guy? (1 mark)
Identify two things that make this guy a bell-end.
    (6 marks)
How can you infer that this book is shit? (8 marks)
Write your own fucking book then. (40 marks)

You would all come up with very different answers, and it would be almost impossible to say which was best.

We all remembered what happened to Ho6. We appealed her results, quibbled back and forth, and proved that her students had, in fact, answered the questions. The results went up from Es and Ds to As and A*s. Heigh-ho, said the Exam Board. Clerical error. Such a shame those gifted students now weren't taking English A Level. Never mind. Maybe they can read books later in life?

We emailed Ho6 to tell her the good news. She was delighted, but maybe that was because she had just drunk a piña colada on the beach in Barbados, a copy of *Middlemarch* nestling in the sand, having finished teaching at an International School at 3 p.m.

The Man from the Exam Board wore the brittle smile of the educational establishment, born of stress, ennui and having to answer the same questions all day.

We began standardisation, which involved eating Jaffa Cakes, drinking coffee and marking anonymous papers to see if we were in line with the Exam Board. Then we argued about whether the anonymous student had correctly inferred what orang-utans were threatened by.

The Man from the Exam Board took almost identical answers and showed us how they could be up to two grades different because of the use of a single connective or linking phrase ('this implies that the orang-utans are like humans' immediately places it in a higher band than 'this shows that the orang-utans are like humans', for instance). As standards had improved across the country, the Exam Board had been forced to become more punitive, and tried to find fault with the smallest things.

English Language GCSE regularly defeated us teachers. We knew the answers, but the jargon to express the ideas kept changing. 'It was much harder in my day' is an old saw no longer used among teachers.

The next day, I had a standardisation meeting about Year 12 which was even more confused. Representatives from all the Exam Boards were there, supposedly helping us understand the new specification we were about to embark on. They all disagreed with each other over the standardisation; in some cases, a Band 1 response was given a Band 5 by a different examiner.

Lesson #520
No One Knows Anything.

I went home and sat at the kitchen table and marked the rest of my papers. The question was: 'Describe a time when you have made a good choice' (40 marks). I kept referring to the mark scheme and the standardisation materials, but couldn't make head or tail of them.

When have I ever made a good choice? How many marks would I give myself for my choices in life? Sometimes it's 12, sometimes 39. Amy came in and I asked her to think of a time when she made a good choice. 'No comment,' she said, and went to bed.

I yawned, and was about to close my MacBook, but thought I should just take a cheeky peek at Facebook. Oooh, hello. Lots of panicked and angry posts from teachers about OFSTED: 'This is a fucking joke. We shouldn't have to do this, not now. It's not like I don't have enough to worry about with exams. I mean, what is the point?'; 'Totally agree, we should all go on strike'; 'Smiley emoji'; 'Two smiley emojis'; 'Ten smiley emojis. See you all tomorrow!!!!!! Xxxxxxx.'

Little Miss Outstanding had written, 'That thing where you should be planning lessons and marking books for an inspection, and you are actually busy finding amusing gifs to make your SMARTboard look pretty . . . lalalala-laaaaa!'

She was clearly crapping herself.

I finally trudged upstairs to the spare room at 1 a.m.

I lay awake for hours.

I should have taught *Catch-22*.

My main goal was to get results. The only way I could get results was for the kids to do practice papers. But if the OFSTED inspector saw them just doing practice papers, then I would be given Inadequate. Which would mean I was a shit teacher. Yet, if I only taught All Singing All Dancing OFSTED lessons, then the OFSTED inspector might come in and give me a Good or Outstanding, but the kids wouldn't do any exam practice, and so would fail their exams. Which would mean I was a shit teacher.

I would be crazy to teach any more lessons, and sane if I didn't; but if I was sane, then I would have to teach.

The lessons passed in anxious torpor.

Nobody came.

YEAR 11, WEDNESDAY, PERIOD 3.

I handed out a coloured flow chart with all the phrases and connectives they needed to know for each question. I wrote Lesson Objectives:

To feedback on homework
To develop skimming and scanning and inference skills
To establish a regular routine of triangulation

Janice said, 'What?'

I said, 'Just do it.'

A man with a clipboard entered, navigated past Rich's knees, and stood at the back of the classroom.

No. Not now. Any time but now.

'Sir, what's triangulation?'

'Well, it's . . . er . . . marking, basically. Which brings me to your work I need to give back. Yes. So, unfortunately nobody did very well. I mean, you did. Or rather, you do. Normally. But this time you didn't.'

He's writing something down.

'Janice, if you could hand them back. So if you look at the papers, I think we all had a problem with the orang-utans and whether or not they were similar to humans. So let's try that question again, but this time ensuring that we infer rather than explain . . .'

'Sir, what is the difference between *explaining* and *inferring*?'

'Well, you see, *explaining* uses words like, erm . . . whereas *inferring* uses words like erm . . .'

He's writing notes. What is he writing? I haven't said anything yet! Oh God, he's looking in their books! *No, no, no!* Not Janice! Hers is one of the only ones I haven't marked! Come on, man! They've been doing practice papers! On paper! He's circling something on his pad.

'What was I saying . . .?' I whispered.

'You were going to tell us the difference between explaining and inferring?'

'Yes, well, explaining, you see, is when you explain something . . .'

They stared at me.

Mr OFSTED held his pen to his lips.

'Sir, what is the meaning . . . what is the *meaning* . . .?'

'Er . . . I used to know this . . .'

'Sir? Are you OK?'

I stared out of the window at the smoking triangular chimney. The Grand Vizier Lizards had their teeth into me and were beaming me up to their spaceship.

'Sorry . . . I used to be able to speak . . . language . . .'

At the end of the lesson, I ran to the toilet. MegaDumper was in there; I hammered on the door, demanding he get out.

I changed as fast as I could and just ran.

And ran.

1 mile – Split: 8.56 minutes per mile . . . He's on the C/D Borderline so you need to target him. I'm on the AC/DC Borderline. I'm UP. Now I'm DOWN . . . I've been down so long it looks like up . . . Sir, what is the difference between explaining and describing and inferring? Sir? SIR? WHAT IS THE DIFFERENCE? . . . I think his inability to speak ENG LANG rendered his lesson INADEQUATE, I would place him on a Cause for Concern OFSTED EDEXCEL MOPCEF Ultrasound . . .

Maybe you can learn to speak English? Data cluster-fuck. A.B – A.B – A.B.C – Year 11 Set 3s are weak . . . *2 miles – Split: 8.7 miles per hour* – Triangulation for the Nation – Discombobulation – Disintegration – Dystopian – It's just Diss – Isn't that in Norfolk? – Nor FUCK – Shuffle – No more – No more Marking – Mark it, nuncle: Have more than thou showest, Speak less than thou knowest . . . Fitter. Happier. More Efficient. Like a gerbil. On a treadmill. On Prozac – Shit, what's wrong with my phone? – Come on – Play – Oh God, I've got to call Apple again – I can never remember my password – How was your Genius session today?

18

Library Fire

I ran in the next morning to find Bill chiselling 'OUT' into the zinc sign.

'Outstanding!' I cried.

'You can't argue with that, can ya?'

The SMs were delighted; they strolled the halls smiling and congratulating teachers. They felt we had reached the Promised Land, and now anything was possible. Among the rest of the staff, however, there a mood of exhausted discontent. Now the focus of OFSTED had been taken away, staff thought about issues they did not have time to address during the rest of the year: changes to the curriculum, cuts, stress, work overload, pay. They spent their free periods searching for jobs and drooling over websites of International Schools, dreaming of other lives.

Every day, there were more rumours. The Doom-mongers were in their element as they spread butter on their toasted pitta bread.

'Have you heard?'

'No, what?'

'Sharon. From Science.'

'No. She's not!'

'Yup.'

'And Brian from Maths.'

'No!'

'Uh-huh.'

'Not to mention Barry the TA.'

'No! He can't!'

'Well, that's it then.'

'We're fucked. Might as well leave.'

Everyone was leaving. *Everyone*. Well, not strictly everyone. Some people. But by the time it had progressed through the Doom-monger Telegraph, it had become everyone. There would be no teachers left. It would just be the Doom-mongers, a bag of pitta bread and some laminated cue cards.

The meeting had to be on the downlow. The emails had gone out to our private emails, rather than our work ones, to maintain secrecy. The Union Rep approached us individually in the playground with a furtive wink.

Meeting, after school. In the Library.

All the unions were going on strike the next day, so the Library was as packed as on a Friday night.

'OK. Before we start, I want to make sure that whatever is said in this room stays in this room,' said Union Rep, like a guerrilla plotting to overthrow a military dictatorship. 'Now, Head is aware of the Strike Action. We had a very constructive meeting.'

'And?'

'No calling out.'

'Order!'

'Mine's a Stella!'

'And . . . it was a very constructive conversation. We met eye to eye, and there is definitely going to be some movement on these issues.'

'Can you be more specific?'

Union Rep looked over his shoulder surreptitiously.

'Not. At. This. Moment. But, as I say, we had a very healthy dialogue. Whoever marches tomorrow will not dock any pay. You will not need to set cover. And it will not affect your reputation.'

'Is the school going to shut?'

'I really pushed for it. Really, I did. But he wouldn't budge.'

Boos and whistles.

'OK, OK, OK. Look, what could I do? Nothing shuts the school. Not snow, not strikes, not anything. The school will stay open and sub teachers will be bussed in. The kids will all be doing practice papers in the gym while we are marching.'

There were some grumbles from the Old Guard, who wanted the school to shut down. The kids needed to have their education disrupted. The parents needed to freak out that their dear progeny might miss some crucial exam preparation. They needed to know that we were working under intolerable conditions.

The sad realisation was that it was probably best for the kids to do practice papers in the gym until the exams. We were no longer needed. The strike was explicitly about the banner issues of pay, cuts and work overload; implicitly, we were protesting out of anxiety at our own obsolescence.

The next morning we all had a good lie-in, watched a bit of *Jeremy Kyle*, had a fry-up and then met at the train station. We gathered in the square, marched along behind some large banners, chanted, and then got back on the train home. We were back in the Library, tucking into pints, before the kids were out of the gym.

'Well, that was underwhelming,' I said.

'That's the Blob for ya,' said HoD. 'By the end of this year, every member of the Blob will be gone, you mark my words. The Death Star sees us as the problem. Under the *ancien régime*, kids were spending all their time in a spliffed-out haze while their loony-lefty teachers promoted deviance, drugs, revolution and homosexuality. We need to be purged.'

A jubilant version of 'Hey Jude' struck up, as HoD asked me what I wanted to do with my sixth formers next year. I told him I was going to do *The Waste Land*. He guffawed.

'Let me guess: you thought studying *The Waste Land* was going to civilise the natives?'

'Something like that.'

'By furnishing them with pretentious quotes to roll out to impress people at dinner parties for the rest of their lives? Eliot was a waste man. And that was some dumb Upanishad he chose. Do Baldwin. They don't need a poem about a depressed right-wing loser wandering around complaining about not getting laid. They need *The Fire Next Time*. They need a fucking fire lit under them.'

'It's a bit difficult to light a fire in a vacuum.'

'Tell me about it. I used to teach upstairs in this mental room with crumbling eaves and crazy crenellations. It's now the Business Studies Suite with zinc carpets. I used to go in there and fucking howl *Howl* at them. We did it all: James Baldwin, Alice Walker, Flannery O'Connor, Thom Gunn, Kurt Vonnegut. It was the nuts.'

He drifted into another reverie about the old days.

'You know that when Baldwin was a teenager he used to walk from Harlem to the New York Public Library every day to read? That's the bit I love about my job. When I tell the kids that, and then I say: go down to the Library and find any book you want. And just read for a double period. Fucking magic. I come down and just browse. I run my fingers along the bookshelves, and pick books at random. I whisper into their ears that what they've got is good, but this one is the one for their eyes only. And they go away and they read that and they are changed for ever.' He belched defiantly. 'We had an English teacher here who had been a pianist on cruise ships. One day he found a copy of *Wide Sargasso Sea* lying around on a deckchair and he read it in one sitting. Made him decide he had to be an English teacher just so he could teach that book. That's what I want in my Department. I don't want TeachFirst, Ask Questions Later. I want Teach Now, Forever. I don't want people who get firsts from Oxbridge. Best teachers I ever met failed their exams. Or they're school drop-outs. Or dyslexics. Wow, they can teach. People who can see things a bit differently, who are imaginative, who understand the struggle of learning, who've got a bit of grit. People don't teach because they think they know it all, but because they realise how little we really know. People who know how precious education is. People who understand that this shit is all there is. I want a school that values people and books.'

'"The vale of soul-making".'

'Yup. Keats knew. The world is a school, and the human heart is the book in that school. Baldwin knew that. Vonnegut knew that. Books are sacred and must never be banned or burnt, in schools or anywhere else. Because that's what's happening. That's right. I heard yesterday that we're closing the fucking Library. That's it! Books? Who needs 'em? You can just Google 'em!'

HoD gulped down his pint and slammed it on the table.

'What do we value? Hmm? Chairs? His chairs, his Bimmer and his screens. Did you see the delivery this week? Another shitload of screens. One screen for every pupil, that's the goal. Ensure they never have to look at a teacher, or into their soul. That's money that should have gone on books for the Library, which he is fucking closing. Fucking scandal. Just click on the link, copy, paste. Turn on, tune out. Go 'puta, go uni, go job – *What do we value?* We used to have assemblies with Nelson Mandela or Noam Chomsky. Now what do we get? Whoever won *The Apprentice*. "This morning, we are going to look at how you can aspire to use your education to make money and suck out your soul. Then when we have dominated you, 95 per cent Arse to Cock, we will send you out ravaged and lobotomised to be supplicant to The Man. To the Soulless Technocracy."'

'You always get all *ubi sunt* after a couple –'

'Don't *ubi sunt* me, you cu–'

'Don't you think there's just a hint of rose-tinted spectacles here?'

'Yeah. Of course there is. I'm getting older and more nostalgic. Whatevs. Look. This is serious. Fewer and fewer kids are doing English. There are hardly any Music teachers being trained. Everyone's doing Science. Great for doctors and engineering, gnads for us.'

'Lots of people want to do Media.'

'Great. Yeah, thanks for that. This is the death of Humanist education, which has been the foundation of education in this country for centuries. We are replacing these robust, tangible pillars with ephemeral clickbait. Soon the school will just be kids at computers all day long, with headphones on, doing the same Maths problem on an online programme until they get it right. You will be even more redundant than you are now. I'm gonna hire some hotshot teachers in China – or even better, a robot AI – who can teach via Skype and download the multiple-choice answers into their facescreens. And you, my friend, can have my poxy job.'

He went quiet.

'No, really. I'm leaving.'

'No!'

'Yup.'

'What are you going to do?'

'Dunno. Fishing. Poetry. Anything but this. I can't do it no more. When you lose that thing with teaching, it's time to move on.'

He always said this. As he himself admitted, he had been about to leave since he arrived. But this time, there was a more profound melancholy to the statement.

'We'll all be gone. Me. That guy. Her. Him. All of us. *Ubi sunt*, indeed.'

Tom sat down next to us, sighing, 'Ah, I've heard this rant before.'

'Where you been?' shouted HoD. 'Havin' a Tommy Tank in the bogs over my *Much Ado* lesson?'

'You wish,' muttered Tom as he looked out of the window.

'Oh, sorry to bore you', HoD huffed. He got up, flashed a glare, and shuffled out of the Library.

After an awkward silence, Tom asked how Amy was doing, then told me that they too were expecting. I hugged him delightedly, then recommended NCT groups and car seats. He apologised for how things had soured between us. I told him I forgave him; we laughed at the notion that we were the only ones left – well, us and the weird Trainee, who was bound to get a job now, no matter how shit he was – so we had to stick together. We said we would get together over the summer. He shook my hand warmly and smiled, his eyes glimmering.

Then it was exams.

Invigilation.

Turn over your papers.

Stare at wall.

Stare at Janice inferring.

Jeremy Kyle game.

Go and stand behind the student most likely to:

> Go to prison.
> Be the first person on Mars.
> Be a bigamist.

More paper.
Five minutes.
Time's up.
PLEASE LEAVE THIS PAGE BLANK.

Back to the Department. More crying kids upset by HoD leaving. And the rest of the Old Guard.

Even Little Miss Outstanding was out of there. It was an unavoidable truth that she was leaving. The cards covered every surface.

'Miss! I can't believe you are leaving! Please take me with you! Please be my teacher forever!!!!'

When I asked where she was going, she mumbled something about a school in the countryside that was really relaxed, but she wouldn't tell me its name. Definitely private, then. Nothing to be ashamed of, I said. They say it's like going from walking on glass to walking on velvet, after all.

At the Final Assembly, Head showed the opening of *The Devil Wears Prada*, in which Meryl Streep comes into the office and everyone changes their shoes, cleans their desks, straightens the flowers. Head said, 'Well, put me in a dress and call me a woman.' I think he thought this was an example of good power. I tuned out after that. I awoke as the samba band were playing 'Gold' by Spandau Ballet. Exit music.

HoD bade us a brief farewell in the Department. He said this wasn't goodbye, and that we were all ring pieces, but that he loved us all and we were the best around. Then he threw Cheese Strings at us and told us to hurry up and get to the Canteen.

The All Staff Leaving Do was so long we had to have an interval. Head tried to say some poignant things, but he was drowned out by applause and shouting.

And so they all went. Brian and Anushka from Maths, Sharon and Stuart from Science, Jill from Art, Gary from ICT, Tony from DT, Ella from RE, Damilola from History, Carol from Drama, Steve from Music, Nick from PE, Dario, Stefan, Anna and Bob from Modern Languages, HoD, Little Miss Outstanding, the Librarian, half the TAs and Learning Mentors. It was like we had pulled the foundations out from under the school. It seemed the only people who weren't leaving were the SMs. And Bill and Paula.

And with that, The Old Guard – a Yoda or a Hector, every one – were disappeared. And with them, it felt like a whole world had gone. We could tell ourselves lies about why they had to go – done my time, family, better salary, need a new challenge, need another language, need a sun tan and a piña colada. Many just wanted to move on to a school that perhaps wasn't so Outstanding, and therefore slightly more human. They had been tipped over the edge by stress and disillusionment with a system that was now out of control. The very system that had improved schools almost beyond measure – from the worst to the best – was now destroying itself from within, like a phoenix whose stomach is burnt out by flaming embers.

Lesson #555
Kids Need Consistency.

To chop and change teachers all the time is discombobulating for staff and pupils alike. High-performing schools get great results, but there tends to be a concomitant high turnover of staff.

Lesson #556
Teachers Must Be Cherished.

The Old Guard provide wisdom and stability. They have relationships with kids that stretch way beyond the classroom – they have taught that kid's brother, so they know how to approach his family; they can take stressed out new teachers under their wings; they have experience of the whirligig and whack-a-mole of the bonkers educational system, so provide valuable perspective; they are more committed to 'passing it on' than with results (although some manage both); they are wise. Like books, they are all too easily taken for granted and tossed on the pyre of relentless, unforgiving progress.

PART THREE

19

Please Leave This Page Blank

I was supposed to be putting the cot up. And the shelves. But the wall is just way too compelling.

It's not just any wall. This wall is my son's *tabula rasa*. The blank sheet upon which his soul will be written.

I could put the shelves up now. Get the books ready.

Goodnight Moon; *Papa, Please Get the Moon for Me*; *Alice In Wonderland*, *Wind in the Willows*, *Winnie the Pooh*; *Charlie and the Chocolate Factory*, *James and the Giant Peach*; Harry Potter, *His Dark Materials*; Greek Myths, *Hamlet*, *To Kill a Mockingbird*, *Of Mice and Men*, Dickinson, *Hamlet*, *The Waste Land* . . .

iPhone, Xbox, dope. Losing the ability to focus and communicate. Ennui. Apathy. Angst. Put books back in storage.

Shit. How are we going to educate him? In the Latin sense: *educare*; to lead out. If education is the 'leading out of what is already there in the pupil's soul', as Miss Jean Brodie says, then it is our job to lead them to realise their own ideas and identities, rather than didactically impose ours upon them. We need to lead him away from this whole benighted culture – the screens, the violence, the misogyny, the pressure, the corruption of innocence. But he must discover the way himself.

We talked about getting out of town, moving to the countryside.

That means I either have to work at a dead-end white-flight school with no aspirations, or a private school. I can't handle the private-school shame. Why can't I go private? It's like going from walking on glass to walking on velvet, after all. Crab sandwiches for lunch. And the holidays are even longer than ours. I could do with an extra two weeks. Could start staring at that wall over there.

Apparently, you teach the *whole* child in a private school. As opposed to what we do, which is teaching a classroom full of amputated torsos and severed heads.

But they're about building character, aren't they? And all that extracurricular malarkey. I could direct them in Greek plays in the amphitheatre, lead mindfulness sessions at lunchtime, take them to Russia. They're all Russian now, after all. Go hang out with the fam in the dacha.

We could live somewhere green and innocent, where we could teach and live and love, unharassed and unobserved.

But I'm not some craven lickspittle paid to grease the palms of an Admissions Tutor, so Piers or Sergey can snort their way through three years of ivory indolence. Where's the challenge? Where's the impact? Once you've changed lives, you can't go back.

We could go away. Everyone left to go away. Away must be good. They speak different languages there, which is bound to be beneficial. Apparently, bilingual kids are smarter. Well, they can speak two languages, for one thing.

Go forth and teach all nations, like Jesus said. We could go to France, Spain, Italy, Germany, South America, Turkey, Dubai, China. Barbados!

And there's no stigma with going private. Go private school in England, become pariah. Go *International* private school, become best friend. Everyone says, 'Great, I'll come see you next summer.' The further you go, the more acceptable the English class system becomes.

Could go back to Tanzania. God, that was the sweet spot, right there. Get up late, do a little bit of 'teaching' in the mornings (reading whatever I wanted), then play football, before repairing to my hut, while I awaited the battalion of sweet, polite kids who came round every evening demanding to know more, waxing lyrical about Harry Potter and *The Gods Must Be Crazy*.

The school had fuck all. No photocopier, limited internet access, tiny classrooms with a corrugated roof covered in fruit bats. No standards, league tables, exams, OFSTED, iPads, Outstanding, Good, Inadequate, no features, no features at all; no data-meetings, twilight INSETs, morning briefings, admin, box-ticking, book-trawls, data-cycles, pupil voice questionnaires, Learning Walks, Cause for Concern; no stress, guilt, fear; no shame.

Could go to India.

I remember that video about the 'Hole in the Wall' we watched when we were training. There was a computer in a hole in the wall of a slum. Soon all the kids were teaching themselves, and each other, how to use it. And how to communicate. Their first English word was 'browse'.

It won't be long before they're straight onto Khan Academy's online tuition, learning everything under the sun, and by the time they're ten they will know more than me.

Fuck that then.

Just put a screen in the wall over there and leave him to it.

I should have stayed in advertising making shitloads selling plastic cheese to the Saudis (despite 98 per cent market share and rampant heart disease).

I've got to step up a gear if I'm going to make some proper moolah. Progress ever upwards through the pay scale. Up the M1, M2 and M3 at 100 mph. I can't pull over on the hard shoulder for a breath of fresh air and an egg sandwich. To be static is to be an obsolescent fossil of the old school, wallowing in tenure, egg on tie, muttering the same old lessons. Oh, that's just him, they all say. Leave him to rot.

Keep on up to SMT. The more power you have, the less teaching you do; eventually, I could teach one hour a week, yet charge around the place telling people how to teach. People who, by necessity, think I'm a complete tosser.

I love teaching. But I hate being a teacher. What to do? What teacher are you?

Just teach. That's all. Don't take any more responsibility. No more than being a teacher and a father. That's all the responsibility in the world.

I was starting to see fractals in the blankness when Amy's waters broke. We walked around the house for a while, doing the breathing thing, and then tried to relax by eating M&Ms and watching Merchant Ivory films, but all that repressed passion delayed my son's arrival somewhat. We should have watched Almodóvar.

Then the quickening; game on.

In the hospital, Amy was cleaved and spavined and finally my son was wrenched into the world against his will, backwards, upside-down, bawling to be returned. He was dumped into a tray and kept under harsh lights and prodded and pinched in a glass box and kept overnight for observations. I looked at him, this first night alone, in the cell he might call the world. Miraculously, he had been thinking before this, his mind already a bound ocean. He had heard me speak of this strange world, full of glass boxes of light surrounded by darkness. Did this live up to his expectation? What were his first impressions of this place? Of me and my strange resemblance? He looked dissatisfied. He must have been conjuring other worlds already, or uploading his consciousness to a host somewhere else.

Don't worry, son. I will lead you out of here.

After a few more tests, he was declared alive. We could take him home.

As we gingerly brought him home in a pram, a bus coughed out four big Puffas. One of the Puffas spat a big green grolly at my feet. I was momentarily terrified: this is the way it ends. Shanked on my way back from my son's delivery into the world.

Then the Puffa looked up at me and said, 'A'right, Sir?'

It was Kieran.

The world suddenly gained weight, as if gravity were more forceful. Life was filled with warmth and joy. Amy and son were all I needed.

We did not sleep much those first few weeks. We would wake up to feed him, and then I watched him sleep. I could sit there for hours. I don't think I've ever seen anything so beautiful.

He lay there, all scrunched up, a crushed apple in the long grass. His features were like an alien: an oval head, with sharp nose and mouth and giant, bulbous eyes. His skin was a whorl of pinks and yellows. Occasionally his arms and legs jerked up and down in a panic – and then he was still, spatchcocked. I kept checking that he was breathing by placing an iPad next to his mouth. As I watched his breath condense on the screen, he seemed to be an alien from another galaxy, acclimatising to his new atmosphere. Who knows where he came from or why – all I knew was that I would do anything to protect this fragile little shrimp.

I held him and read to him, even though he did not seem to understand. I walked around the park with him clasped to my breast and told him stories about the world around us – of sunrises and sunsets, plants and flowers, pedestrian crossings and wheelie bins. I felt sure his tiny reptilian brain could understand what I was saying in some prehistoric way. I was forced in these narratives to face up to my own ignorance. A good teacher is always learning. Why can we see the moon in the daytime? When is the best time to plant an apple tree? Where is his other shoe?

I realised I had to undo it all and see the world like a child, pointing and gasping in wonder, babbling free-form, jumping up and down at the sheer joy of it all.

As my son grew, the world invaded his nascent conscious-ness. We lay awake to the sound of his cries. Amy could bear it no longer. She put the pillow over her head and curled up into the foetal position, while I put him in the car and drove him around and around, listening to an old mix tape. Only Old Skool House would put him to sleep.

Sometimes I feel like throwing my hands up in the air. . .

I drove until ten or eleven at night, because I knew that as soon as I stopped the music and turned off the engine, he would start crying again. I wondered why my little alien could not cope with the atmosphere of this world. Perhaps I should just keep driving, onwards and upwards. Out of the town, up the motorway, up and up until I reach a coast, a place that is cool and windy and cleansed, where the sea rolls deep and moody and otters dance across the beach.

As I drove round the corner, I saw Kieran being pinned up against the wall by the police outside Bananaman's coffee shop.

I drove around and around the environs of the school, the windows of the estates and terraced houses lit by a phosphorescent glow.

This is my community.

These kids are my responsibility.

I've got to see them through.

You've got the love I need to see me through . . .

20

Personal Statement

When I went back to school at the beginning of my third year, Mentor was Head of Department, Tom was Second in Department, and Trainee was an NQT. He came in that first day in a sensible suit and a full USB. Good man.

I was a Teacher Without Portfolio. I could finally just teach. I saw Head around, but he proved himself as unable to acknowledge my son's birth as my father's death. Well, he was busy. He had a load of new staff to train.

I was tired the whole time, but happy. My Form were beginning Year 13, their final year, and I was excited about seeing them over the finish line.

'The most important thing is that you sound like you. Not like anyone else.'

They hid behind their computer screens, which pulsed with blankness. This was proving the most challenging assignment of their entire school career. For on this blank pro forma they had to project themselves. Crystallise their very essence.

'The university professors say that every year they get thousands of statements which sound like they have been written by a focus group,' I said. 'Which, in many ways, they have. The clue is in the name: this is your *Personal*

Statement. It has to be unique. It has to properly express who you really are.'

'But, Sir: what if we don't know who we are?' said Liam.

'Google it.'

'I tried. Nuffing came up.'

'I can't help you with that one, Liam. Just pretend you know. That's what life is all about. OK, let's work on these opening lines. Can you capture their attention? Give it a go. You've got five minutes.'

Stares. Coughs. Sighs.

The 7-step Plan for Writing a Decent Personal Statement did not seem to be helping. Indeed, it seemed to be producing a kind of existential horror, as they realised that the exceptionalism we had drummed into them needed proof, and that they were, on paper, very similar to every other seventeen-year-old in the country. With a minute to go, they hurriedly wrote a sentence or two.

'OK. Time's up. Let's hear some of these. Someone we don't often hear from: Zainab.'

Zainab shook her head.

'Come on, Zainab! You're going to have to speak soon. You're going to be sitting in a university interview. Are you just going to sit there in silence?'

Zainab nodded. I told her that I wished she would speak, because her essays were incredible, like the one she had just done for me. I said that she must do English at university. She said she wished she could, but that she was going to have to give it up. I fell to my knees and pretended to beat my head on the floor.

'Noooo! Why?'

'My parents don't want me to do it.'

'What do they want?' I asked, rhetorically.

'Become a doctor,' we both said, simultaneously.

I pleaded with her to reconsider, but she was resolute. I picked myself off the floor.

'Anyone else? Liam?'

Liam cleared his throat and opened his arms, as if performing an aria.

'I have been interested in mortgages since a very young age. I was fascinated to know how mortgages work, and what consumers needed to do in order to get one.'

He awaited applause.

'Have you really, Liam?' I asked.

'What?'

'Been interested in mortgages since a very young age?'

'Yeah.'

'You mean instead of playing football and climbing trees you were studying mortgages?'

'Uh-huh. What, Sir? It says here: "Make sure you express your passion for your subject."'

'Yeah, but don't lie!'

'I ain't lying. Swear down.'

This morning was supposed to be for them to finish it off. Just tweak them. We had been trying to establish who they were and what they cared about every morning for weeks, and we were still on the first line. Their extra-curricular section was particularly weak. All the private-school kids did a gazillion impressive things – they walked across Afghanistan and learned Mandarin and played violin to grade 8. The universities claimed they weren't interested in anything beyond the subject any more, but it was clear extra-curricular gubbins still gave the private-school kids an advantage. It certainly gave them confidence, which was the most important attribute when going into an interview.

I asked them to write down their ideas.

'OK. Let's hear some of these. Ella?'

'One thing I done is that I organised the coconut shy at my primary school.'

'That was a while ago though, wasn't it? Have you done anything since then?'

'Nah.'

'Well, maybe just cut the word "primary". That's called being economical with the truth.'

I perched on the desk, shaking my head.

'I don't get it. Look at you all. You've been given this incredible education. Do you *only* want to make money?'

Nods around the room, apart from Alexia and Zainab.

'What about teaching?' I asked. 'Anyone want to be a teacher?'

Widespread derision.

'Nah way, Sir!'

'Bare jokes!'

And then I said it. The thing I swore I would never say.

'In my day –'

Mother. This has to stop!

Ella cut me off.

'Yeah, yeah. In your day, you would put books on our heads to make you stand up straight.'

'Yeah, and bells on our foreskins to stop you – yaknow-whatImean?'

'Ugh! Liam! That's gross.'

I launched into an impromptu fogeyish rant about the death of Humanism.

'Humanism! Isn't that what university is for? Reading as many books as you can, from the greatest minds that ever thought. The best words in the best order. Who said that, Liam?'

'Lady Gaga?'

'This is why you need books, Liam. The bedrock of our civilisation. To spend the next oh-so precious time in your life marinading in the history of ideas. And then you can become a mortgage adviser . . .'

Liam laughed in my face.

'Yeah, but, Sir, it was all right for you, wasn't it? You didn't have to pay off the debt. I would love to be able to spend three or four years free of charge just reading books.'

'Liam: you have spent the last year singularly failing to read two books, so forgive me if I find that an extremely dubious claim.'

'But, Sir! What's the point?'

'The point, Liam, is that this is our culture. Without this, you don't exist. You don't have a soul.'

'Nah, sir. This stuff is dead. Finito. Mortgages *is* culture.'

'Unfortunately, you are absolutely right. Which is why we are going to hell in a handbasket.'

I googled David Foster Wallace's Kenyon Address from 2005 and put it on the board. I told them that they had a lifetime of deadening routine ahead of them, and English was the only subject that would get them to fifty years old without having put a bullet in their heads. That English was about attention and consciousness, which were as endangered as libraries, trees or teachers. That the alternative is 'unconsciousness, the default setting, the rat race, the constant gnawing sense of having had, and lost, some infinite thing'.

Liam went 'Woooaahh.'

Ella said, 'Sir's dark.'

The bell went.

'OK, off you go. And remember: you only miss the shots you don't take.'

'Wayne Gretzky!' shouted Liam, suddenly very animated.

That year, I was doing lots more new stuff, which is what you want. Keeps you fresh. *Jekyll and Hyde* with Year 9s. Donnie had come up another set to Set 2. He had already made an origami model of a Victorian street, so I let him do some Show and Tell. I did *The Crucible* with Year 11s. We had already set the scene for the Salem Witch Trials: misogyny, irrationality, fear, mob rule. We did some McCarthy context, but it was all going on, right outside the window, all around. And, of course, *The Waste Land* with the 13s.

I had said, many times, that *The Waste Land* was the most important poetic work of the twentieth century. (I don't think I sounded very convincing. I'm not sure I thought this. But lots of other clever people did, so I thought I should parrot the notion.) We read it through twice, and it didn't make any sense whatsoever. They all agreed that *The Waste Land* was just waste, man. I had tried everything. I started with the iPad edition. We watched Fiona Shaw performing it and Jeanette Winterson discussing it. I photocopied *The Golden Bough* and we read Isis and Osiris, and the Fisher King. *Nada*.

I spent my evenings reading and rereading the poem trying to find a route in. I finally submitted to the path of least resistance: sex. We talked about Eliot's unusual living arrangement with Vivienne Haigh-Wood and Bertrand Russell, but then every essay Wally wrote was about how the poem was an expression of Eliot's sexual frustration because 'his mate Russell was having it off with his wife in the next room'. (I was on strict instructions to keep an eye on Wally's sexual improprieties, since he sent Mentor an email saying, 'Miss, what was the homework? x.' We studied that kiss for a long time. I said it was probably fine, just the way people naturally sign off a message. 'Ugh,' she said. 'Gross. Just keep him away from me. And females generally.')

We compared the poem with rap lyrics, but they just took the piss out of me for that; it committed the Cardinal Sin of trying to be Down with the Kids. I was risking losing them altogether.

There was nothing for it. We were going to have to join up with Tom's class and do a performance.

They weren't happy. It was enough of a wrench to get them to perform it to each other, let alone to Tom's class, who were much cooler. Alexia and Ella read the salty, mouthy music-hall barflies, Zainab 'read' the suitably silent Madame Sosostris, Liam was a desperate Phlebas drowning under coats. And it was all rounded off with a feeble, and out of sync, rendition of 'London Bridge Is Falling Down'.

After the reading, I asked both classes what they heard. They were silent. They still thought it was mystifying, dull and irrelevant.

I told them I had heard things that I hadn't before. They still kept shtum.

Lesson #697
Admitting That You Do Not Understand Is a
Great Leveller and Pays Great Dividends.

At times like this, you have to level with them. I said I felt frustrated by the poem – I thought it was great but now wasn't sure. Maybe, just maybe, it was all a load of old cobblers. I pointed to the Eliot quote on the wall – 'Genuine poetry communicates before it is understood' – and Keats's definition of Negative Capability. I tried to help them understand that they needed to undo themselves, to dismantle their analytical apparatus. We had to get past the alarm that would go off when they looked at a line, an alarm that then disabled their minds and told them that they didn't understand any of it. It was healthy to be in doubt and confusion. We did not have to reach after an absolute answer. What Eliot was getting at could be beyond data and even language.

For the Plenary, I wearily asked, one last time, what they had heard. Anything. They started to tentatively offer ideas: 'environment', 'destruction', 'connection', 'community', 'alienation'.

Boom ting.

I charged out on duty.

Yes!

Breakthrough!

Come ON!

I charged around the playground, punching the air. I noticed VP staring at me, so I came to a standstill and put my hands behind my back, and gave her a salute. I breathed out deep foggy breaths and patted my hands against my coat, then walked in purposeful circles, past the other teachers on duty, muttering, 'Chilly!' or 'Blimey!' or 'Should have worn the leggings!'

Skip. Skip. Skip. Skip. Skip.

There's that kid again. The one with the haircut that looks like a loaf of bread. And that one – the one with the crazy deep-blue eyes. Those have to be lenses. Nod to that History teacher who is always late on duty.

My legs are churning, but I maintain outward grace. I am a swan. Zen Zeus.

A ball flew over the cage. I kicked back a curling cross, which landed perfectly on the lanky Year 11s's head. They all cheered.

Zen Zeus Zidane.

I realised Salim was standing next to me, hands thrust deep into his pockets, beanie hat pulled far too far down his forehead, toes pointing inwards. We stood for a while, looking around in contented silence. I looked at the great leafless horse chestnut trees with the conkers beneath them like fallen Christmas baubles. It was such a nostalgic sight, conjuring childhood memories of a hundred

breaks and lunchtimes, of string and vinegar and five-ers.
I picked up a conker and turned it round in my hand.

'What is that?' he asked.

'That, Salim, is a conker.'

'What does it do?'

'Well, Salim, this is . . .'

What the fuck is a conker?

'It's a . . . well, a . . . a, you know . . .'

'No. What is it?'

'It's a . . . a seed! Yup, that's right. It's a baby tree. A big
acorn.'

'Oh.'

'And in my day, we used to put string through them
and varnish them in vinegar and then have competitions
where you had to knock the other kid's conker off the
string.'

'Why?'

'Well, because it was fun.'

'Why?'

'Because you got to knock the other conker off and
that showed that you had the biggest and best conker.
It's Social Darwinism, basically. "He who has the longest
stick will knock down the most persimmons."'

'What's a persimmon?'

Why did I say that?

'It's like a plum.'

'What's Social Darwinism?'

'The idea that you are born with the biggest conker.
Or stick. So you either have it, or you don't. So you must
stay in the same place in which you are born. You cannot

improve yourself in any way, say through education. What do you think of that idea?'

He shrugged.

Skip. Skip. Skip.

Gradually, almost imperceptibly, one of his feet started to shuffle. Back and forward, back and forward, the soles of his Clarks dragging across the concrete in a smooth moonwalk.

'Are you dancing?' I asked.

'Yes, Sir.'

'That looks like a great dance. Is there any more?'

'Yes, Sir.'

His arms cut the air, while his whole torso flexed and his hips writhed. It was a startling unspooling of silky movement. I said I wished he had told me he was a world-famous Bollywood star. I realised VP was eye-balling me and gesturing for me to circulate, so I per-ambulated, like an Edwardian consumptive taking the air, walking round and around, feigning interest in the utterly repetitive.

Skip. Skip. Skip. Skip. Skip.

A ball slammed into my head. An unfeasibly tall boy held up his unfeasibly massive hands and said, 'Sorry, Sir!'

Wow, those Year 10s are getting sweaty. Glad I don't have them next lesson. Oh shit, here comes Head. Head down. Walk with purpose. Grimace.

'Sir.'

He addressed me! That's a first. Called me Sir!

'Ahem. Hi.'

Skip. Skip. Skip.

The blue electric neon clock clicked from 10.19 to 10.20; the flirty History teacher turned on her heel with a wink; Salim shuffled back and forth; Mercedes skipped over the skipping rope; Donnie carried his origami model carefully across the playground; VP nodded for me to wind it all up. As the great chaotic murmuration was swept into order, I felt my chakras aligning and marvelled at the unity and rhythm of the universe.

Who knew *The Waste Man* could be so uplifting?

Lesson #711
When This job Is Shit, It's Hideous.
But When You Have a Breakthrough,
There's Nothing Like It.

What a job! The infinite variety! Every day I am a shapeshifter. I transmute from teacher to parent to therapist to sociologist to director to actor to game-show host to data manager to policeman to prison guard to alchemist to guru to arsehole to God to human. I am all of these things and none of them. I am whatever they decide I am.

Teaching is one of our few natural functions, which we discover as we grow. We cannot escape it. The humanity, the nurturing, the joy of discovery. It is all we are here for.

21

Alexia

She still wouldn't say a damned word. Kept quiet the whole lesson. She was starting to annoy me.

From the Starter through to the Plenary, she never put her hand up or offered her ideas, even though she could destroy us all. In group work, she drew out the best of her group – enabling them to speak and annotate the text and encouraging their ideas – without ever telling them what she thought. She was a guileful, subtle teacher. Far better than me. I often invited her to teach the class, but she demurred, so I had to bang on myself.

After a double lesson one afternoon, I asked her why she never said anything, to which she replied she didn't know. I told her she had to stop being so humble, that we were all desperate to hear her ideas. She said she felt weird speaking in class. I accused her of doing everyone a disservice – I think I went as far as to say she was neglecting her role as a Senior Student – it was her *job* to tell us, to show the rest of the class what an A* response sounded like; to *model* the way to think about literature.

She said she found *The Waste Man* too difficult to talk about.

'I know it's difficult –' I said.

'No, it's not that it's difficult. It's that it's difficult to talk *about*. I find it overwhelming. It's . . . shattering.'

Oh.

OH.

OK.

Then out of nowhere, she said, 'You know when all our faces are blank and we're all looking out the window?'

I knew that sensation only too well.

'It's because you said something really deep and it's sinking in.'

I was struck dumb. You reach a stage with teaching where you think back on lessons, and you have just been going through the motions. Delivering. Facilitating. And yet, there are those wonderful moments scattered through the week where you go off on a tangent, or give them a personal anecdote, and you say something they never forget.

Lesson #808
They Remember the Tangents.

'Yesterday,' she said, 'when you said that thing about Kubrick. How he had said, "The most terrifying fact about the universe is not that it is hostile but that it is indifferent." And how we have to find our own meaning, our own light in the vast darkness.'

Who'd have thought it? Perhaps Meedja wasn't so useless after all.

Having puffed me up, she then knocked me down. She pointed out a mistake I had made. I asked her why she didn't tell me at the time; she said, 'I didn't want to disrupt the class.' I said, 'That's what we need! That's what makes my life worth living! We need disruptors! For God's sake, the world is full of all these idiots who call themselves disruptors. We are crying out for a genuinely intelligent disruptor.'

Gradually, the disruption began. I could see her straining at the bit. She could do the essays in her sleep, and she got full marks for almost all of them. When I printed them off and handed them out for the rest of the class to Peer Assess, she sighed and told me to put them in the bin. She was frustrated by the formulaic nature of the essay mark schemes – we had to teach them to crowbar Assessment Objectives into their essays, giving them allotted marks for AO3 (critics) and AO4 (context), for instance. She had devised an essay formula, a paragraph formula, a sentence formula, and that was all there was to it. But English wasn't Maths – it couldn't fit into boxes this way. The mark schemes didn't demand that she approach the texts on their terms. She started producing essays that were cynical in the way they knowingly undermined the tick-box expectations. She was in danger of self-destructing.

To begin with, she didn't care much for *The Waste Man*; it was too patriarchal, canonical, full of nonsense. Then Tom and I took a trip to the Globe to see a celebrated production of *The Tempest* by an experimental Eastern European company. I was wary since the trip to Oxford – not to mention the trip to see *The Crucible* in the suburbs where the actors blacked up – but I was sure this was a winner. It was youthful, dynamic, physical, and with an angry contemporary political dimension. If they wrote about this in the exam, they would surely get maximum brownie points.

When we reached London Bridge, Tom told them he had a secret mission. But it wasn't compulsory. Indeed, he wouldn't advise it at all.

This is how to negotiate with kids. It's like my piano teacher said: If you want kids to play the piano, lock up the piano. Or you want to get a great essay on *Wide Sargasso Sea*, make them read *Jane Eyre*, then mention off-hand after a lesson that there is a really dangerous, sexy, radical version set in the Caribbean, but we don't have time for that now.

We recited:

Unreal City,
Under the brown fog of a winter dawn,
A crowd flowed over London Bridge, so many,
I had not thought death had undone so many.

They were cringing with embarrassment.

Tom lectured them about the different eras of the city, and made them try to guess when each building had been built. We walked across the bridge into the oncoming tide of commuters and, a century on, it was still the case that 'each man fixed his eyes before his feet'. Or rather, their phones. Tom challenged the kids to make eye contact with more than three people between the start and end of the bridge. The City boys couldn't believe their luck when all these young women started giving them the eye. Alexia was totally game, unlike adults would have been.

Suddenly, she came out of her shell and was connecting with every commuter, bringing them out of their prison.

Then we went to Tate Modern and stood on the bridge over the Turbine Hall. Tom told them to imagine being a child in this wide cavernous space and Alexia ran down and encouraged the rest of them to roll down the giant ramp. It was impudent and childish, and they did it without shame.

At the Globe, we had to be groundlings, which meant standing up and getting 'bare cold'. The 'physical theatre' element of the play was predominant; it wasn't long before naked people were waving dustsheets, writhing and playing freeform jazz, shouting in a strange language. Prospero was portrayed as an incontinent, Ariel as a pill head, and Caliban as a member of the Taliban. The play had been heavily edited; some of Shakespeare's imperishable language appeared on screens, but we were groundlings, so we missed most of it.

On the train back – after I had swept the carriage for suspicious characters – we agreed that we shouldn't do anything cultural ever again.

But I assured them that reading the play would be different. Like *The Waste Man*, there was a way to make this real. To make it ours.

Once *The Waste Man* clicked, Alexia fell for Modernism hard.

She was enthralled by Virginia Woolf; every time I walked past her, she was reading a different book: *Dalloway* in the Library, *To the Lighthouse* in the Canteen, *Or-*

lando on the picnic table, *A Room of One's Own* in the Common Room. It was infectious. The other students across the year saw her reading, and wanted to read too, because she was a high-achieving Senior Student who was also humble. Everyone liked and respected her. She talked to Ella about how she could link the superficialities of Jazz Age New York to the London of *Dalloway*; to Zainab about feminism and the stream-of-consciousness technique; she discussed Baldwin and Ellison with Isaac at lunchtime; she put a copy of *The Golden Notebook* in the Common Room. Alexia set up a book club after school and invited writers to come into school (which the SMs tried to block, but we worked out how to smuggle them in). She made reading cool.

And so the books took root within them and the great flourishing began. Day by day, page by page, they learned to own the texts and to trust their own minds. We sat in the denuded Library, picking the last precious leaves off the tree.

I no longer had to do much in class. Most lessons they taught each other. And it was during one of these lessons, in which I sat back and listened to the babble of contented learning, that Mentor came in and observed. I panicked. I had no slides, no Lesson Objectives – I hastily made some up – 'to teach each other', 'to read', 'to live in another world'. She decided it was Outstanding. The irony. The lesson in which I prepared and did the least was deemed the best.

I was done. I had taught them to teach themselves, and therefore had realised my inbuilt obsolescence. I could begin the process of self-destruction.

Soon, Alexia was bossing it in class too: leading the discussion, giving presentations on Woolf's experiments with time, style, mundanities. She became interested in how Woolf's vision of a Modernist landscape is fundamentally an optimistic one – there is the possibility of a better world in her work, and you can see how it might be brought about. She compared Woolf's optimism with Eliot's pessimism. The whole class argued about who was the most depressing; in the end, most felt that Eliot and Woolf were, in fact, uplifting, and that they had become more positive and enriched since reading them.

Boom ting.

When I finally asked her for a title, she found it difficult to be specific. She said she wanted to do something about modernity and progress and the Theory of Relativity and how Woolf played with the disconnect between real time and inner time. I suggested 'Progress Over Time'.

She began editing a Feminist Magazine with Zainab and a couple of other girls from her year. She dyed her hair blue.

I told her she had to try for Oxbridge. She asked why.

'Because you're more than capable enough,' I said.

'But I want to be a social worker,' she said. 'Why do I need to go to university at all?'

'Because you'll be doing what you love.'

She said she doubted herself too much – not just her talent, but the value of the degree itself.

'What is the utility in doing a degree in literature in this day and age? I could better spend my time and money –

lots of it – studying something with immediate real-world applicability.'

I told her it didn't matter, it was means-tested, she wouldn't have to pay anything, or very little. She still didn't like the sound of it, all those posh, arrogant, cloistered Toryboys. Luckily, she met up with an Old Girl who had gone up the year before, who was humble, grounded and happy. She was convinced.

Alexia's greatest transformation came during her preparations for her Oxford interview. We discussed poems one on one, and did some mock interviews. At one point, I asked her – rhetorically, but perhaps to allay my own doubts – why she wanted to study English. What was the point in the modern age? She said that nothing could be more relevant – at its most basic, what is English but the ability to absorb and analyse media? What skill could be more important in this world where the internet and the real world no longer seem separable? She said the medium was not only the message, but the whole universe. She talked passionately about how she wanted to go to Oxford because she needed to be challenged. She wanted to plunge further into Literary Theory, and to produce radical reinterpretations of patriarchal, canonical texts. She was committed to the new politics of identity – gender, race and sexuality had never been more significant. I said that was great, but that Literary Theory was like heroin. I'd seen some of the greatest minds of my generation hooked on that junk. They never thought or wrote clearly again.

I asked her why she didn't want to do History or PPE or an Ology.

'Because I am interested in the inner life. Literature has never been more vital. It is about understanding how we see the world in which we live. And how others see it. And how to make the world better. But more because of the love of it. The love of books. The love of life. The love of some infinite thing.'

Apparently, she didn't say any of that in her actual interview. I asked what she did say. She just shrugged and said, 'Oh, you know.'

Zainab didn't say anything in her interview, so didn't get in. She was fine about it all. She could go to Bristol and be happy. Wally didn't do any preparation, but was lucky enough to have a room next to the tutors who were interviewing him, so he heard them discussing his interview the night before, and crammed all night. He got in.

Alexia sat down next to me in the Library one afternoon and started taking about her essay, and then said, as an afterthought, that she had got in. I jumped up and tried to hug her. She shrugged. Too cool for school.

22

You Taught Me Language

'You know, iambic pentameter.'

'You're a what?'

'What?' I said. 'Iambic pentameter.'

'What are you?'

'I'm not anything.' I said, 'Iambic pentameter.'

'You're a bit what?'

'You know. Like the heartbeat. Like all that stuff we did. *Da-dum-da-dum-da-dum*.'

'*Da-dum-da-dum-da*-don't.'

'Let's read it again:'

> But this rough magic
> I here abjure, and when I have required
> Some heavenly music, which even now I do,
> To work mine end upon their senses that
> This airy charm is for, I'll break my staff,
> Bury it certain fathoms in the earth,
> And deeper than did ever plummet sound
> I'll drown my book.

'What is he doing here?'

'Drowning his book.'

'What else?'

'Dunno.'

'Anyone?

'Anyone?

'Bueller?'

I was going to finish *The Tempest* if it killed me. I couldn't believe that we were finally reaching the end and still Ella didn't get iambic pentameter.

The bell went.

The exam season brought relief; after the constant obsession, the mocks, the predictions, the strategising, they were finally upon us. GCSE and A Level students went on leave, so I barely saw them. Occasionally, they popped up to revise between exams.

The school had emptied out, so felt more like summer camp. My timetable had freed up; I wandered around, peering over kids' shoulders as they revised, offering pithy asides like 'Too late now'. Zainab and Alexia read over their highlighted tomes; Liam was lodged at the computer, frantically scouring SparkNotes; Wally pretended that it was all fine, and that he was spending his exam leave in the pub; Ella tried to get me to have her registered as dyslexic, so she could have extra time.

In the last couple of weeks, the English teachers shared out revision sessions. We tried to keep them as relaxed as possible by bringing in Jaffa Cakes and organising games, quizzes, lectures and seminars led by the kids.

In our last session, I was overcome with sadness. They had all worked so hard, and come so far. We had time for only a brief discussion about age, fathers, daughters,

honesty, hubris, tragedy, nature, colonialism, art, what
might be the exam, and what they would do for the rest of
their lives, before the bell went. All the English teachers
wrote poems for them, which were mostly riffs on what
we had been studying.

Let you go then, you and I,
With your summer holidays
spread out against the sky
Like a patient revising upon a picnic table

The kids stuck their final Post-its on the way out as we
wished them Godspeed.

I walked out of school with Liam.
'Please tell me you'll do some work, Liam,' I said.
'I will, Sir.'
'And you won't spend the next week playing World of
Warcraft.'
'No, Sir.'
'But that's what you said for the mock, and look what
happened there.'
'I was young, Sir.'
He winked at me and went into his house.
I looked through the Post-its in my pocket.
'HOORAY!'
'DONE WITH SCHOOL FOREVER!'
'Laters.'
'Thanks, Sir.'

The night before the exam, I lay in bed, racked with nerves.

Fuck. What if nature doesn't come up? Or colonialism? Or art?

I should have done more on magic.

I should have done more of everything.

There's so much I have not told them.

Lesson #1001
You've Never Done Enough.
You Are Never Done.

Oh God. Oh God. What if . . . *what if* . . . what if I have been teaching them the wrong thing all along? Like the completely wrong play. Maybe the paper will be about *The Merchant of Venice*. Then what would they do?

Sue me.

They wouldn't do that.

Would they?

I've had them for two years. We have an understanding.

They've driven me nuts, but I already miss them.

I really like them. They're like my friends now.

I never told them what they mean to me.

I arrived long before the exam began to put all the papers out on the desks, just repressing the urge to sneak a peak.

When the kids arrived, I took a paper register and gathered in their textbooks. Alexia was Zen, Zainab looked terrified, Wally diffident, and Ella chaotic. Ella said, 'Nah, please, Sir, just one more minute!' as she flicked through the Introduction to the Arden Edition one last time. Liam arrived as they were filing into the gym.

They sat at their desks.

Stillness.

A hand went up for paper.

I took the red marker and put the time they would finish on the board, as well as the time for those with extra time. I cleared my throat and commanded, with the solemnity of a priest performing last rites, 'Begin.' (The rest of your lives.)

I perched on the desk at the front and opened the paper.

It was a gift. A gift! Such brilliant questions! Women. Colonialism. Art. Authorship.

It was all there.

Phew.

All my lot started to scribble spidery essay plans.

Go for it! They're going to nail it.

I stood like a statue for the hour; a statue who occasionally walked, with stately authority, from one side of the gym to the other. And back again. As I walked around, I caught glimpses of what they were writing. Zainab had planned it all perfectly, but was thrown when her turquoise pen started leaking. She looked really panicked from then on; her handwriting became less than perfect, almost skittish. Not as skittish as Wally, who rested his head in the crook of his elbow, and scribbled like a life-support machine of a patient going into cardiac arrest. Isaac was all over the place, but he got something down, at least. Ella wrote slowly, but her plan had at least two quotes on it, so I breathed easier. I caught Liam's eye. He smiled, winked and made the 'Luminati symbol at me.

Have I illuminated? There is so much I haven't told them. A whole universe.

At the end of the exam, they ran out into the playground and signed each other's shirts giddily.

Alexia was worried. She said she deviated from the essay formula, and from her essay plan. Wally had filled the pages, and was nodding incessantly, saying, 'Nailed it.'

'How did it go, Ella?' I asked.

'Yeah. Pretty well.'

Oh dear. That means it was a disaster.

'And you, Liam? You seemed to be getting stuck in?'

'I wrote, like, bare pages.'

'And you answered both sections?'

'Er . . .'

'Oh God, Liam.'

'Got you there!'

'"Prithee, nuncle, keep a schoolmaster that can teach thy fool to lie".'

'Wassat?'

'Nothing, Liam. Nothing. Nothing at all.'

'See you at the ball, Sir!'

And then there was only joy. The sun shone on the girls dancing and the boys playing cricket at lunchtime. Whenever I walked past on my way to lunch, Mick was pretending he could bat. A boy bowled him out, followed by a great melee as the other fielders wrestled each other for the bat. I bowled a few balls at them, which tended to be smashed onto the roof. It didn't take long for an SM to ban cricket, because the boys were becoming unbearably sweaty and smelly for their afternoon lessons.

The sun blazed down on Sports Day. It looked like a medieval jousting tournament. White lines had been drawn on the parched grass; flags fluttered; marquees were fixed to the ground; an ambulance parked near the podium; lines of eager children sat cross-legged in red shorts and blue aertex shirts. One by one, they leapt up as their names were blared from loudhailers and assumed the starting positions. An air of triumphant, final release.

I had hoped I might get recognised with one of the 'glamour' roles on Sports Day: medal giver; cameraman; starting-pistol firer. I got Toilet Duty.

The Toilet is in a brown brick bungalow in the middle of the park. The heat made it even more stinky than normal. I sat outside that shit-shack all afternoon.

Not everyone can go toilet at once. It just isn't feasible. Imagine. The whole school going toilet. That would be chaos. There was a system. Each form got a laminated card. Only one child from each form could go at once. If a child wanted to go toilet, they had to take said laminated card and give it to me.

'Can I go toilet?'

'Do you have a card?'

'No.'

'You have to have a card.'

'Oh, Sir, but please. I'm bursting.'

'I'm sorry, but rules is rules. You've got to have a Toilet pass to go toilet.'

'Please, Sir. Please. I ran the hundred and then I drank a whole Capri Sun. Please!'

I let the child go toilet. The child handed me the card when he came out.

On a day when they were very excited and had been drinking free Capri Sun all day, they definitely didn't go toilet properly. And they definitely didn't wash their hands properly. By the end of the day I had most of the school's wee on my hands.

As the afternoon wore on, I noticed the smell sweeten to the unmistakable scent of sensimilla. Mercedes had been gone a long time and not come back. I knocked on the door of the Ladies.

'Hey! Put that out! Now!'

A gruff voice replied, 'A'right, Sir.'

'Mercedes?'

'Sir?'

'Come out here now.'

She emerged sheepishly.

'You are in a lot of trouble, young lady.'

'Oh, please, Sir! Please, Sir! Please don't tell nobody!'

'I have to tell somebody! It's my job to tell somebody!'

'But I didn't do nuffing wrong!'

'You were smoking weed in the toilets!'

'Yeah, but this is a park. It ain't school.'

She had me there.

'This is a school event and you are committing a heinous crime!'

'Wassat mean!'

'It means this is a criminal offence!'

'Please, Sir! If I get 'scluded again it will be permanent. I'll never be able to come back to school. Please. I'm begging you. Look, I'll use AFOREST. (Whassa-first-one?) Oh, yeah, Alliteration: Please Please Please. F?'

'Fact.'

'Fact: I ain't done nuffing wrong. Den what is it?'

'Opinion.'

'Opinion: I don't fink I done nuffing wrong. I definitely don't fink I done nuffing wrong. Den what?'

'R. Rhetorical Question.'

'Do you fink I done nuffing wrong? No. Didn't fink so. Den?'

'E, Emotional Language.'

She pretended to cry.

'Boo hoo, please, Sir! Please! My heart is breaking! Don't 'sclude me! If you do den I'll be on the streets –'

'Smoking weed in the park toilets?'

'Zackly! Den?'

'Statistic.'

'Statistic: 99 per cent of people who get 'scluded is unfair.'

'And how much of your brain is destroyed by this stuff?'

'0.000000001 per cent. And den it is . . . wait don't tell me . . . TRIPLE! TRIPLE! TRIPLE! OK: you won't regret it because you are the biggest, bestest, most butters teacher in the world.'

'Get back over there.'

'Ooh, yeah! I got two hundred metres!'

She ran off, tripping over her laces.

Salim sidled up to me.

'How you doing, Salim? You need to go toilet?'

'Nah.'

'Just come for a chat?'

'I guess.'

'Did you compete in anything?'

'Javelin.'

'How did you do?'

'So are we going to do a dance at the end-of-year Assembly?' he asked.

'Look, Salim. I don't think –'

'I've worked out a whole routine.'

'Oh, yeah?'

'Yeah. Do you want to learn it?'

'Sure. Why not? Got nothing better to do.'

He looked around, shiftily, to check no one was looking, then pulled his beanie hat down, gathered himself and unleashed a killer set of moves.

'So this is the Head Scratcher . . . and this is the Does My Belt Fit . . . and this is the Hell Yeah It Does.'

'Wow. Wow.'

'Come on, Sir! Your turn!'

'OK.'

We danced. Soon a crowd had gathered around us. I heard someone whisper, 'Dat is bare embarrassing.'

My severe persona undone in a moment. But what did I care? He was happy and confident, and such a dude.

'So is this it, Salim? Anything else?'

'No, we just need to get some roller skates.'

'OK.'

'And then at the end we are going to abseil down the gym wall.'

'Of course we are. What have you got planned for the summer?'

'Got to learn a lot of new moves.'

'Can't wait to see them next year. Take care, Salim.'

He shuffled off home.

As I left the park, I saw Head reprimanding the new Head of Year 8 for running with a girl to the finish line in order to encourage her. 'That was totally inappropriate' was all I heard him say.

After school, I opened up my email.


```
Dear teachers
  You have been a real pleasure to me this
year and I am so happy with my self. Thank
```

you so much Paula and Sir and Miss and
Miss. I hope every one of you have a lovely
summer holiday and of course don't stress
yourself with work do have some holiday so
thank very much.

Thank you all

Donnie

You are the best teachers

Thank you

The end-of-year Assembly was renamed 'The Schoscars'.
Olive trees stood at each corner of the gym draped in fairy
lights. On the screens scrolled images of black-and-white
film stars. The SMs looked awkward in ill-fitting suits and
dresses. Head gave out prizes in a white tux ('The next
prize goes to a young girl – you wouldn't know, to look
at her, that not only is she a *refugee*, but she has just been
diagnosed with M.E.! Unbelievable! Give her a big hand!')

Mentor gave a special prize.

'This is an award that recognises the person who maxi-
mises their potential, curiously, wondering where their
true potential will take them. And if you're this young
person, your true potential has taken you to an extraordinary level of achievement. This individual stays behind
every day to do extra work. Recently, he made a model
of Victorian London out of origami. This person should
know that they are not only an inspiration to their peers,
but an inspiration to all their teachers too. This person is
Donnie Jones.'

Donnie shook the hands of the SMs, then stood awkwardly to acknowledge the rapturous applause. He was proud, but not as proud as I was. I could not see his dad anywhere.

'And to sing us out, here's another of our stellar students to sing a stellar song.'

Mercedes belted out 'Happy' with the Gospel Choir.

At the Leavers' Ball, Isaac DJ'd some dirty grime. The whole year was a melee of bumps, grinds, hugs and kisses. VP stood on a chair and segued effortlessly between the 'Big Fish Little Fish Cardboard Box' dance move and the 'Keep Six Inches Apart' gesture. My form made a circle around me, and jumped up and down. Even Zainab. Liam was dancing so vigorously that I said, 'What have you been drinking?'

'ENERGY DRINKS, SIR! That's all I ever drink. My body is a temple!'

'Yeah, right,' I said.

'True say, Sir. Swear down. Aks anyone. Dis shubz is sick! Come on, Sir! Time for some old school moves!'

I hit the floor for a quick Hell Yeah It Does, a dangerous whirligig of flailing limbs and awkward staccato head thrusts, like a giraffe on Ritalin falling down the stairs. Liam filmed me on his phone. Go, Sir!

This role model. This sweaty man, unencumbered of any dignified carapace. This happy man.

I patted them on the back and told them they were amazing and I would never forget them.

'Good luck in Thailand, Wally.'

'Thanks, Sir.'

'Don't do anything I wouldn't do.'

'Liam: give me a ring once you've reached that Dungeon Run. But not before. Seen?'

'Seen, Sir.'

'Ella: I'm gonna miss you.'

'Gonna miss you, Sir! And a little word of advice: you need to sort out your ties!'

'Kids have been telling me that since the beginning.'

'Zainab: I'm very disappointed that you gave up English, but I am relieved the medical establishment is getting such a star.'

'Thanks, Sir.'

'Alexia: when you are prime minister, give us a pay rise.'

She handed me an antique copy of *Murder in the Cathedral*, which she had inscribed 'Thank you'.

Head swept onto the floor and danced with the Head Girl. The kids went nuts, and started filming it on their phones, cheering wildly. Soon the rest of the staff joined in.

I walked back to pick up my jacket from the back of my chair. A few of the sixth formers were sat, staring at the table, as VP told them a joke.

What did the tank commander say to his men before going into battle?

Silence.

Get in the tank.

Silence.

I saluted her, and headed for the exit, where Liam, drenched in sweat and energy drinks, staggered into me.

I asked to see his video. 'Sozzles Squazzles, Sir. I already Snapchatted it! It's gone! Boom!'

I left before too many awkward sweaty goodbyes. Tom, Mentor and I got a cab home; we laughed all the way home about all the funny confessions kids had made to us, and how great they had all been (in stark contrast to the rampant misbehaviour of the teachers).

'What a crazy job,' I said, as I got out of the cab.

'See you on the morrow, bright-eyed and bushy-tailed!' said Mentor.

I tried to open my front door as quietly as I could, but my son woke as I tiptoed up the stairs. He mewed listlessly for a while; I picked him up from his cot and bounced him on my knee and shushed him. I reached down and picked up the board book next to the bed. He nestled under my armpit as I read *Papa, Please Get the Moon for Me* as quietly as I could.

It is about a man who gets a big ladder and climbs up it. He takes the moon, and brings it down to earth to give to his daughter.

Occasionally, my son reached over and batted the page with his hands, and gurgled his appreciation. When I finished, he looked up at me and grunted.

I read it again.

And again.

GLOSSARY

A Level	Course taken over two years between sixteen and eighteen. Students usually take three subjects
AFL	Assessment For Learning
AO1, AO2, AO3, AO4, AO5	Assessment Objectives. Used as marking guidelines for teachers
BH	Behaviour
BTEC	Vocational qualification
Chalk and Talk	The Old School practice of standing at the board and talking about your subject, occasionally with recourse to using chalk in order to write things down
Circle Time	A time in the day when disruptive pupils convene with mentors or SEN specialists
CW	Coursework
DEAR	Drop Everything and Read
DT	Design Technology
EAL	English as an Additional Language
Future Leader	A leadership programme for School Leaders

GCSE	Course taken between the ages of fourteen and sixteen. Students are examined in around ten subjects
GTP	General Teacher Programme
ICT	Information and Communication Technology
INSET	A preparatory course, taken at the beginning of each term or year, which usually lasts between one and three days
NQT	Newly Qualified Teacher
OFSTED	Office for Standards in Education
PE	Physical Education
PEE	Point. Evidence. Explanation.
Peer Assessment (abbrev. Peer Ass)	When pupils swap books and mark each other's work
PGCE	Post Graduate Certificate in Education
PPE	Politics, Philosophy and Economics: undergraduate degree at Oxford
PTA	Parent Teacher Association
RE	Religious Education
S&L	Speaking and Listening
Schools Direct	The most recent training programme for new teachers
SEN	Special Educational Needs
SM	Senior Manager
SMT	Senior Management

TA	Teaching Assistant
TeachFirst	Teacher Training which places high-flying young graduates in schools in deprived areas
UMS	Uniform Mark Scheme
VA	Value Added. A school's quality is now judged on how much value is added to their students, ie. how much they have improved
VAK	Visual, Aural. Kinaesthetic. Some constituent parts of a well-differentiated lesson

Amazeballs (*adj.*)
Amazing; incredible (*mostly posho*)
'That lesson I just taught was totes amazeballs.'

Bantosaurus (*n.*)
Someone with exceptional bantz, unusually from PE

Bantz (*n.*)
Banter; chat; repartee; badinage
'That new PE teacher gave me good bantz at break.'

Differentiation (*n.*)
Differentiate (*vb*)
The means by which a teacher assesses different kinds of learners in the classroom

Douchebag (*n.*) (abbrev. **douche**)
Idiot; fool; moron (origin: vaginal cleaner)
'Move your books off my desk, douchebag.'
'Aren't you supposed to be teaching, douche?'

Emosh (*adj.*)
Emotional (*posho*)

Ring Piece (*n.*) (abbrev. **Ring**)
Bum-hole, arsehole, anus, rectum, sphincter, brown eye,
chocolate starfish, Gary Glitter, rusty sheriff's badge
'Liam is a bit of a Ring Piece.'
'Kieran is a total Ring.'

Tommy Tank (*n.*)
Wank (*rhyming slang*)

Totes (*adv.*)
Totally (*mostly posho*)

Aks (*vb*)
Ask
'Are you aksing me?'
'I aksed you if I could hand it in on Friday.'

Allow it/'Low it (*phrase*)
To leave something alone; don't worry about it
'Sir! I gave it in! Allow it!'
'Low it, I ain't doin dat.'
'Sir, can we set fire to our hair? Allow it!'

Badman (*n.*)
Rudeboy; gangster; rebel; scallywag
'Sir, Kieran is copying! Do your own work, badman!'

Badman (*adj.*)
Naughty
'Sir, you need to put dem badman mandems in detention.'

Bare (*adj.*)
A lot of; very
'Rah, we got bare homework, you know.'
'Dere's bare bears on dere.'
'Dat cupboard is bare bare.'

Blud (*n.*)
Mate

Boom ting (*phrase*)
(Also: **Buff ting**)
The best; amazing; beautiful
'Rah, I got an A! Boom ting!'
'Dat girl is buff ting.'

Bruv (*n.*)
Brother; Confrere
'Yeah, bruv, what you sayin, bruv, nuffsaid bruv, yes bruv,
innit bruv.'

Butters (*adj.*)
Ugly
'Sir's lookin bare butters today.'
'Dis lasagne is butters.'

Beatdowns (*phrase*)
Beaten up
'Man's going to get beatdowns.'

Bwuk up (*phrase*)
Ibid.

Comeden (*phrase*)
Come on then; Let us make haste
'Man goin Mafs. Comeden.'

Dat (*n.*)
That

Fam (*n.*)
One's peoples; someone you consider family
'*Where was you in Mafs, fam?*'

Izzit dough (*phrase*)
Is it, though?; Are you certain that is the case?
'*I was in Mafs.*'
'*Izzit dough?*'

Laters (*int.*)
Goodbye

Limpix (*n.*)
The Olympics

Lol (*acronym*)
Laughing out loud (also written occasionally as 'Lots
of Laughs'), used as a brief acronym to denote great
amusement in chat conversations
'*Sir knows you wuz bunkin Mafs, lol!*'

'Luminati (*n.*)
The Illuminati (pl. Lat. *Illuminatus*, 'the enlightened')
Various secret societies who conspire to control world
affairs, by masterminding events or placing agents in
position of power, in order to establish New World Order
See also: **'spiracy**.

Mafs (*n.*)
Mathematics

Man (*pron.*)
Me; you; one; the system
'Man's got bare homework.'
'Man gotta go toilet.'
'The Man is watching you.'
'Stick it to The Man.'

Mandem (*n.*)
People; one's tribe
'Dere was bare mandems at shubz on Friday. Two mandem came on tandem.'

Megalolz (*superl. phrase*)
Extreme amusement
'Mandem fell off tandem! Megalolz!'

Moist (*adj.*)
Bad; idiotic; embarrassing
'Dis book is moist.'
'Don't say dat, you are bare moist!'

Oh, my daze (*phrase*)
Oh my days! My goodness!
'Oh my daze, you are bare moist!'

Old School (*adj.*)
Old; retro; back in the day
'*Some old school Super Mario bizzness.*'
'*T. S. Eliot is so old school.*'

Old Skool (*n.*)
A type of dance music from the 1990s
'*Dis Old Skool is old school.*'

Rah (*int.*)
Goodness

Run tings (*phrase*)
In control
'*Man gonna play in midfield and just run tings.*'

Safe (*adj.*)
Cool

Seen (*interrog./affirm.*)
Do you understand?; to acknowledge something
'*I'm going playground, blud. Seen?*'
'*Seen.*'

Shank (*vb*)
To stab
'*Mandems gonna get shanked at shubz.*'

Shubz (*n.*)
Party

Sick (*adj.*)
Brilliant
"Low it, dat's gonna be some sick shubz."

'Slebrity (*n.*)
Celebrity

Sozzles (*n.*)
Sorry
'Sozzles, man forgot homework.'

'Spiracy (*n.*)
Conspiracy
'It's all a 'spiracy. All of it.'

Sozzlesquazzles (*n.*)
Very sorry
'Sozzlesquazzles, man forgot homework again.'

Swagger (*n.*)
Cool
'Sir ain't got no swagger.'

Swear down (*phrase*)
I promise. (*emphatic*)

True say (*phrase*)
I concur

Umfing (*n.*)
Um . . . a thing . . .; delaying tactic when you don't know the answer

Wa'gwan (*phrase, greeting*)
Hello. How are you today? What is happening?

Waste (*adj.*)
Excreta; in need of excretion; superfluous in terms of space, time or life; pointless; draining; poor; bad; nasty
'*Dis lesson is waste.*'
'*Da Waste Land is waste, man.*'

Wavy (*adj.*)
Drunk
'*Sir was gettin' bare wavy on Friday wiv Miss.*'

What you sayin'? (*phrase*)
How are you doing today?

Zackly (*adv.*)
Exactly